Roscoe of Liverpool

His Life, Writings and Treasures

1753 - 1831

by

Donald A. Macnaughton
M.A. (Oxon)

formerly Vicar of Berwick-upon-Tweed
and
Hon. Canon of the Cathedral of St. Nicholas,
Newcastle-upon-Tyne

By the same author:

*

A Highland Family:
The Macnaughtons of Remony,
1780 - 1930

*

There's no town like Berwick

*

In a Fair Ground, A Chaplaincy in Provence

First published 1996 by Countyvise Limited, 1 & 3 Grove Road, Rock Ferry, Birkenhead, Wirral, Merseyside L42 3XS in conjunction with the author Donald A. Macnaughton.

Contents

Roscoe of Liverpool

Preface

In his lifetime William Roscoe was much admired for his gifts and universally respected for his integrity by the people of Liverpool. It is not surprising that Henry, his son and biographer, and others, who have written about him since, have done so in eulogistic terms. Times have changed. William Roscoe has become a half-forgotten legendary figure, despite the fact that streets are still called after him in Liverpool and London. From being a real person living in a vibrant eighteenth century society at a time of revolutionary change, he is today regarded by many of his critics with curiosity and pity as a victim of outdated ideas and has been reduced to the status of an oddity or even a fraud. This trendy reductionism, so rife in our times, can so easily distort and diminish the past.

William Roscoe was in fact a pioneer in many concerns which are especially relevant in the last days of the twentieth century, freedom from oppression, justice, peace, parliamentary reform, penal reform as well as education, literature and the arts. His interests were so diverse that a definitive biography, which would do him justice, might be expected to occupy the best part of ten years of research and preparation. My modest work on the Life, Writings and Treasures of William Roscoe is intended for the general reader and not the specialist, in the hope someone may be encouraged to produce a more comprehensive work which would do him full justice.

The primary source for any work on Roscoe consists of the two volume Life of William Roscoe, by his son, Henry, compiled and published within less than two years of his father's death. This work has long been out of print, is somewhat tedious to read but full of valuable information not easily obtained elsewhere. The other principal sources are the Roscoe Papers, at the Liverpool Record Office, comprising a mass of correspondence over a long period, and Roscoe's own published writings.

William Roscoe had his weaknesses as well as his strengths and I have been careful to mention some of the former, though I am old fashioned enough to believe it to be more important to dwell on the positive virtues and achievements of those who have gone before us than on their vices and shortcomings.

I want to thank all those who have assisted me in the preparation of this book and especially those who have provided me with literature and information, among them Dr Cecil Clough of the Liverpool University History Department and Mr Edward Morris of the Walker Art Gallery, and not least my wife, Diana, for her encouragement and unfailing help.

I am also grateful to those who have granted me permission to illustrate this book with copies of works in their possession, notably the Board of Trustees of the National Museums and Galleries on Merseyside, the Staatliche Museum in Berlin and the National Gallery of Art, Washington, and the Liverpool Athenaeum.

Donald A Macnaughton

Roscoe Surrounded By His Books
from the painting by Sir Martin Archer Shee
in the Walker Art Gallery, Liverpool

Chapter One

Man of Many Talents

Observant visitors to the Walker Art Gallery in Liverpool will have noticed two large portraits facing each other across the main staircase. These men were contemporary, men of vision who dreamed dreams. Napoleon is seen, with an air of grim determination, advancing across the Alps on his mule, a man of war, aspiring to become an emperor after the manner of Charlemagne. William Roscoe, whose ambition was to be a patron of the arts in Liverpool in the style of Lorenzo de'Medici in fifteenth century Florence, and who was to gain an international reputation for scholarship, is seen surrounded by his books in the privacy of his study in the town he loved so well and scarcely ever left.

In a letter, written in 1799, to Lady Holland, Roscoe complaining about 'the hindrance to their literary commission to Florence' caused by the Napoleonic War, said that he does not know 'whether the Gaul or the Russian conqueror is the most hostile to whatever is connected with arts and letters'.[1] Perhaps it would be better to hang 'the Gaul' and Roscoe in different rooms!

Our concern is to unravel the mystery of how a man of humble birth, having no formal education beyond the age of eleven, became regarded as an authority on all manner of subjects, not only in Europe and America but as far afield as India - so much so that people from every walk of life came to consult the oracle, to seek advice or to pick his brains.

Only a few months before his death in 1831, Roscoe, finding himself unable to concentrate on more serious pursuits, set himself the task of 'tracing for the eye of a friend a brief narrative of the principal events of his life'.[2] Failing health caused him to abandon the project, but not before he had recorded some reminiscences of childhood. Otherwise we would know nothing of his early days.

---

1   Roscoe Papers 2111 - Letter to Lady Elizabeth Holland in 1799. H.A.L. Fisher in his 'History of Europe', 1936, page 827, tells us that Suvorov, 'a meteor out of the windswept Steppes, a peasant general, very old, very small and very fiery' led a highly successful campaign in Northern Italy sending 'the little Franco-Italian republics clattering to the ground like a pack of cards' in August, 1799.

2   Life of William Roscoe, by his son, Henry 1833, vol.1, p.6.

1

The house in which Mr. Roscoe was born.

Used by Mr. Roscoe as a crest.

A chair constructed from a beam
of the house in which the poet was born, and occupied by the
Earl of Sefton, President at the Roscoe Centenary.

William Roscoe was born on March 8th 1753 at the Old Bowling Green House, a popular tavern on Mount Pleasant, on a site near the corner of Hope Street and close to the present Roman Catholic Metropolitan Cathedral. Within a year of his birth the family moved house to a new and larger inn nearby, to which was attached an extensive market garden.[3] William Roscoe's father is described by his grandson, Henry, as a man below the middle stature, but of remarkable bodily strength and activity; of much vitality of temperament and greatly attached to field sports and other amusements, for which his son seldom displayed much taste.[4] Roscoe inherited his tremendous energy from his father.

His mother had a very significant part to play in his early education, instilling a lively interest in literature and poetry, encouraging him not only to read a periodical entitled the 'Library in Prose and Verse' but also to learn selected pieces by heart, thus supplementing the basic grounding in the three Rs at school. Roscoe tells us that from young childhood he developed an aversion to compulsion and restraint.[5] He could remember being carried to a school-mistress by a servant with a rod, not without much struggling and opposition, and this happened when he was still wearing petticoats before 'he had the honour of being breeched' - that is, allowed the privilege of wearing trousers. This aversion to oppression in every shape or form remained with him all his life.

Roscoe never forgot the occasion when he and a school-fellow were caned for whipping a top a few moments before the beginning of afternoon school.[6] Unlike other boys, who always tried to escape after a few strokes, Roscoe provoked his master by standing his ground, thus receiving more than his share of punishment.

Neither master nor boy bore any ill-will towards each other afterwards.

---

3   'Roscoeana' by F.W. Dunston, p.31.

Roscoe's eldest son, William Stanley, left a manuscript, in his own hand writing informing us 'that the name of Roscoe seems peculiar to Lancashire... probably of northern origin, as I have seen a town called Roscoe marked on a map of Sweden, (almost certainly a Viking name). He goes on to say 'Many of our family were yeomen holding land and cultivating it themselves'.

4   Life of W.R. Vol.1, p.4.

5   Life of W.R. Vol.1, p.7.

6   Life of W.R. Vol.1, pp.8 and 9.

Roscoe drew a sharp distinction between 'the shameful and indecent method of flogging prevalent in England' in the XVIIIth century and caning as a mode of correction. Roscoe was much concerned with penal reform in later life.

At the age of twelve Roscoe left school seemingly without regrets. Throughout his life he was fortunate in meeting and making friends with the right people at the right time. Before leaving school he struck up a friendship with Hugh Mulligan, an engraver and painter, employed in a chinaware factory next door to his home. Mulligan became 'a kind of mentor to his youthful years', interesting him in design and painting and allowing him to assist in work at the factory.[7] This practical experience stood him in good stead. Roscoe also was able to make himself a book-case with folding doors to accommodate his growing library, which included The Works of William Shakespeare, The Spectator and the poems of Mrs Catherine Philips, entitled 'The Matchless Orinda', a volume given him at the age of fourteen and which he treasured all his life.[8]

Only two boyhood adventures are recorded, both of which shed some light on Roscoe's character. As a teenager he often walked alone in the countryside and on one occasion, when strolling absent-mindedly along the shore of the Mersey, he was cut off by the tide and, being unable to swim, managed with difficulty to ford the waters and reach safety. On another occasion, deciding on a sudden impulse, to emulate his father as a sportsman, Roscoe borrowed a gun and set off gallantly on a hunting expedition. The first thing he saw was an unfortunate thrush, perched on the branch of a tree. With deadly aim he brought it down to the ground and was so horrified by the agonies suffered by the bird, that he never went out shooting again.

After leaving school, Roscoe spent three of the happiest years of his life 'assisting his father in his agricultural concerns', the chief of which consisted of producing early potatoes, carrying them on his head to market in large baskets and selling them 'at very advanced prices'.[9] He also enjoyed looking after the garden, spending his leisure hours reading. His early interest in gardens, plants and flowers continued throughout his life. There is a curious resemblance between Roscoe's account of his early days and

---

7   Life of W.R. Vol.1, pp.10 and 11.

8   Life of W.R. Vol.1, pp.10 and 11.

9   Life of W.R. Vol.1, p.12.

    G.W. Mathews, William Roscoe, p.11. The Potato Market was at this date situated at the top of Lord Street.

his description of the childhood of Alexander Pope, the poet of whom he was a great admirer. This description formed part of his 'New Life of the Author' which was included in Roscoe's edition of the 'Works of Alexander Pope, Esq.' published in 1824 in London.

At the age of fifteen, after working for a brief spell in a bookshop, Roscoe became articled to John Eyes, a young solicitor, for a period of six years. This was the beginning of what Roscoe described in an account of his early days, written in 1831 shortly before his death, 'as the most painful part of my life'. His experience of the seamy side of Liverpool life in the 1760s, at the tender age of sixteen, made a lasting impression on him and is best described in his own words:-[10]

'After residing for a year with my parents, according to a stipulation in my articles, I was sent to board at the expence of my master with his sister, the wife of a captain in the African (slave) trade, who had retired on his savings. I had not been domesticated there long before I was disturbed at midnight by cries and shrieks proceeding from the bedchamber of the captain and his wife. When rushing into the room, I found the captain struggling to get through the window, restrained only by his wife, who was nearly exhausted by the effort. Our joint efforts prevailed, however, to retain him in the room, when he proceeded to put on his clothes and taking a candle in his hand, set out on an excursion to visit his neighbours ... after having knocked to no purpose at the doors till a late hour in the morning he returned home. The immediate cause of this disturbance was a fear of being seized by the press-gang, there being at that time a rumour of a war on account of the Falklands' Islands, but the true tho' remoter cause was the habit he had unfortunately acquired of drinking ardent spirits, which brought on their usual effects, precluding all possibility of his carrying on his profession, but prevented him from giving me the instruction I was entitled to expect from him, and a long attendance on him in his last illness occupied the chief part of my time. In the meantime I passed all the hours I had to spare in perusing such authors as fell in my way, among whom Shenstone was my great favourite, till admiring I began to imitate him.'

---

10 Roscoe Papers No 3925, Picton Library which consists of a Draft Letter, written by Roscoe to his sister-in-law, Mrs Moss, in 1831 shortly before his death, telling the story of his early life.

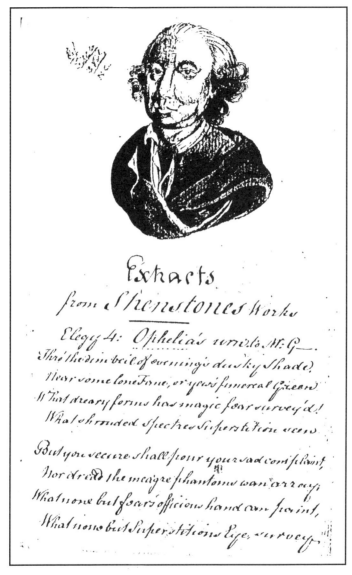

William Shenstone, 1714-63, Roscoe's favourite poet
- 'admiring I began to imitate him' from 'Select Poems from Several
Authors', 1770, Vol 1 page 3. Mss written in his own hand by Roscoe at
age of seventeen as are the drawings.

Evidently, the contract, entered into to enable Roscoe to become an articled clerk, included certain stipulations, one of which appears to have been that Roscoe be provided with board and lodging at the house of Mr Eyes' sister and retired sea captain husband at the expense of Mr Eyes himself. Clearly it was part of the agreement that Mr Eyes' sister and the retired sea-captain act in loco parentis. This ensured the presence of a third person in the house in the event of an emergency. This clever arrangement terminated abruptly on the death not only of the sea-captain, but also of Mr Eyes himself at the age of thirty, described by Roscoe as 'an unfortunate victim of intemperance, no less a martyr to his own misconduct than his unhappy relative'.[11] Roscoe in the same letter wrote down and crossed out a reference to Mr Eyes' failure to afford him any instruction as a clerk. Evidently Roscoe, out of loyalty to his former master of sixty years ago, had second thoughts about criticising him in writing. Henry Roscoe, in his biography of his father, refers to Mr Eyes' death without mentioning its cause. In this letter, written shortly before his death, Roscoe gives us further details of his experiences in the household of Mr Eyes' sister and brother-in-law. 'On another occasion I (Roscoe at the age of sixteen) prevented him (the sea captain) completing an attempt he was making to destroy himself by cutting his throat, in which he had in part succeeded.'[12] These experiences haunted Roscoe until his dying day. This was one of Roscoe's first experiences 'of an anxious and troublesome profession.'[13] He served the rest of his articles with an eminent attorney, Mr Peter Ellames, who greatly appreciated Roscoe's industry at work as well as his literary talents.[14] Roscoe was free to return to his own home, where he continued to live with his sister and father until his marriage in 1781.

During his clerkship Roscoe struck up a close friendship with Francis Holden, who was an assistant at a school in Liverpool run by the latter's uncle. Francis was an outstandingly versatile and gifted young man, so much so that Roscoe found himself comparing his accomplishments with

---

11 Roscoe Papers 3925.
12 Roscoe Papers No. 3925.
13 Life of W.R. Vol.1, pp.13 and 14.
14 Life of W.R. Vol.1, pp.17 and 18.

those of the 'Admirable Crichton'. Roscoe became a lifelong admirer of youthful prodigies. The Scottish historian, P.F. Tytler in his 'Life of the Admirable Crichton', tells us that there were 'other eminent young men, who nearly equalled and in some points surpassed the extraordinary and universal talents of Crichton', citing Angelo Poliziano, friend of Lorenzo de'Medici and tutor of Lorenzo's sons, as an example.[15] Tytler in drawing attention to Poliziano's poem, the Jousting of Giulano de'Medici, written at the age of fourteen, quotes a comment made by Roscoe on the same poem in his Life of Lorenzo de'Medici.[16]

Holden first gave Roscoe lessons in French and proceeded to teach him Latin, helping him to embark on a study of the classics. Two others, William Clarke and Richard Lowndes joined in these studies, forming a group, which met early every morning before the day's work. Francis Holden was away for a time at Glasgow University and later in France. The group continued to meet regularly and grew in numbers. Holden on his return from abroad encouraged Roscoe to learn Italian, thus enabling him to commence his Italian studies for which he became famous.

Holden and Roscoe kept closely in touch during Holden's absence, exchanging precocious and affected letters. In one of these, Holden, on settling in at Glasgow University in 1772, wrote enthusiastically about his life there, telling of the encouragement readily given by the professors and the opportunities for recreation including French fencing lessons, dancing and the Broadsword.[17] He goes on to say:- "the ladies here (Glasgow) have deservedly the reputation of being the handsomest in Scotland ... 'Tis droll to see and hear the concert of Caledonian bagpipes - I fear I weary you - you're not fond of moosick!" Music was evidently not one of Roscoe's strong points.

Roscoe was greatly saddened when his friend Holden, with whom he kept up a regular correspondence until August, 1782, died of tuberculosis

---

15 P.F. Tytler, Life of the Admirable Crichton, Edinburgh 1823, p.24.

16 P.F. Tytler, Life of the Admirable Crichton, Edinburgh, 1823, p.249.

Crichton, educated at St. Andrew's University, at the age of seventeen went to Paris in 1577, where he disputed on scientific questions in twelve languages. After service in the French army, he visited Genoa, Venice and Padua, where he challenged the university in discussion. The circumstances of his early death are shrouded in mystery. He was killed at the age of twenty-three in a brawl at Mantua either accidentally or deliberately. See P.F. Tytler, Life of the Admirable Crichton, pp.76 and 77.

17 Roscoe Papers - Picton Library 2052.

a few months later at the age of thirty. An even greater shock occurred in 1773 when a member of the group, Robert Rigby, aged twenty, was drowned whilst crossing the Irish Channel. Roscoe paid him a tribute in two poems written soon after his death, the one entitled 'To Robert Rigby' and the other - 'Elegy to Mr R.'.[18] Three members of this study group suffered untimely deaths.

In his early days Roscoe was influenced by two distinct circles of friends. There was the group of academic friends, who introduced him to the classics, the Italian language and literature. He was also associated with another circle of friends as a young member of the Unitarian Dissenters' Chapel at Benn's Garden in Liverpool, the forerunner of the Renshaw Street Chapel.[19] The minister from 1763 to 1770 was the Rev. Dr William Enfield, whose sermons were 'almost exclusively those of a moral preacher', and who took an interest in Roscoe, giving him every encouragement.[20] One of Roscoe's earliest writings consisted of a volume in manuscript entitled 'Christian Morality as contained in the Precepts of the New Testament'. In his introduction, the first of many, he carefully explained - 'the object of the ensuing sheets is to collect in one uniform and regular system the moral duties which are inculcated in various parts of the New Testament, by the direct and immediate words of our Saviour, and thereby to promote the knowledge and practice of virtue, and to render the study of the Scriptures more easy and pleasant.' This volume was submitted to Dr. Enfield as soon as it was completed and was returned with a few corrections and comments. Roscoe treasured this volume throughout his life and shortly before his death added a note - 'Done when I was very young, very erroneous and imperfect'. Dr. Enfield was appointed Rector of the Warrington Dissenters' Academy in 1770 and we know that Roscoe visited the Academy from time to time.[21] Weekly meetings were held there at which visitors were made welcome and shared 'the spirit of

---

18 George Chandler - William Roscoe of Liverpool 1953 - Poems from
    Manuscripts of William Roscoe pages 256 and 283.

19 L. Aikin, Memoir of John Aikin (1823)1, 300: Biographical Account of the late
    Rev. Dr Enfield, Roscoeana by W. Dunston, p.30.

20 Life of W.R. Vol.1 pp.36 and 37. Henry Roscoe's daughter, Harriet, married Dr Edward
    Enfield, described as 'one of the moneyers of the Mint', grandson of the Rev. Dr. William
    Enfield who showed kindness to William Roscoe and also appreciated Roscoe's poem
    'Mount Pleasant' as well as his early work 'Christian Morality'.

21 L. Aikin, Memoir of John Aikin, 1 pp.96-98 and note.

companionship and rational enquiry which prevailed there.'[22] Roscoe and
Dr. Enfield's son were both articled to the same attorney, Mr. Eyes, for a
time. Dr. Enfield and the association with the Warrington Academy had a
powerful influence on Roscoe in his formative years.[23]

Roscoe's friendships were not confined to his own sex. He became
acquainted with three sisters from Westmorland, who paid frequent visits to
Liverpool, one of whom, Maria Done, shared his literary interests and became
a close friend and correspondent. Roscoe's first published poem, 'Mount
Pleasant', was originally dedicated to her, but the dedication did not appear
at the time of publication, presumably because Maria had by that time become
engaged to John Barton, who later became associated with Roscoe in the
movement for the Abolition of Slavery. Whatever its merits may be as a
poem, 'Mount Pleasant', as well as giving us a vivid picture of Liverpool
and its surroundings in the late 1770s, includes a robust denunciation of the
slave trade and searching thoughts on luxury, exploitation, and trade in
general:-[24]

How numerous now her thronging buildings rise!

What varied objects strike the wandering eyes!

Where rise yon masts her crowded navies ride,

And the broad rampire checks the beating tide;

Along the beach her spacious streets extend,

Her areas open, and her spires ascend;

In loud confusion mingled sounds arise,

The docks re-echoing with the seamen's cries,

The massy hammer sounding from afar,

The bell slow-tolling, and the rattling car;

And thundering oft the cannon's horrid roar,

In lessening echoes dies along the shore.

---

22   L. Aikin, The Works of A.L. Barbauld (1825) pp.27 and 168-172.

23   J.E. Graham, The Political Ideas and Activities of William Roscoe, 1787-1801,
     M.A. Thesis 1970, New Sydney Jones Library, Liverpool University, page IV.

24   George Chandler, William Roscoe of Liverpool, 1953 p.330.

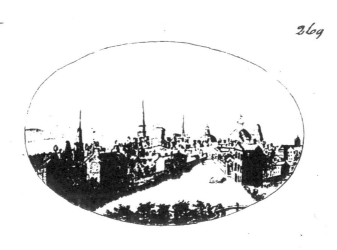

269

MOUNT PLEASANT

A POEM

inscribed to MARIA.

by W. Roscoe.

Easd of the cares that daily throng my breast,
Again beneath my native shades I rest;
These native shades, where oft' I won't to stray
Ere fancy bow'd to reasons bow'led away.

Outside cover of
Roscoe's first published poem, 'Mount Pleasant'.

* * * * *

There with the genuine glow of COMMERCE fir'd
Her anxious votaries plod the streets untir'd;

* * * * *

Shame to mankind! But shame to BRITONS most,
Who all the sweets of liberty can boast;
Yet deaf to every human claim, deny
That bliss to others, which themselves enjoy:
Life's bitter draught with harsher bitter fill,
Blast every joy, and add to every ill;
The trembling limbs with galling iron bind,
Nor loose the heavier bondage of the mind.

Yet whence these horrors? this inhuman rage
That brands with blackest infamy the age?
Is it, our varied interests disagree,
And BRITAIN sinks if AFRIC's sons be free?

Blest were the days ere Foreign Climes were known,
Our wants contracted and our wealth our own,
When Health could crown and Innocence endear,
The temperate meal, that cost no eye a tear:
Our drink, the beverage of the chrystal flood,
- Not madly purchas'd by a brother's blood -
Ere the wide spreading ills of Trade began
Or Luxury trampled on the rights of Man.

Roscoe, rightly proud of his first published poems, sent copies to Sir Joshua Reynolds, who warmly congratulated him on his efforts.

At the age of twenty, Roscoe in 1773 along with a group of enthusiasts, formed a 'Society for the Encouragement of the Arts, Painting and Design'.[25]

---

25 Life of W.R. Volume 1, p.30.

At the inaugural meeting Roscoe recited an ode written for the occasion, described by the Monthly Review critic (December 1774) as 'pretty and ingenious'. The following year the society organised the first exhibition of paintings ever to be held in Liverpool or any English town outside London.[26] The exhibition consisted mostly of pictures by local artists, among them Matthew Gregson and Charles Eyes, whose plan of Liverpool in 1725 was shown. One item appeared in the name of Mr. William Roscoe, Jnr, No. 45 - 'The Mother', a drawing in Indian ink, after a French engraving.[27] Eight years later Roscoe and his friends started another society, the object of which was to educate the public taste through lectures, the first of which he delivered himself on November 7th, 1783. A year later an exhibition was arranged which included paintings by H. Fuseli, Stothard, Angelica Kauffman and Sir Joshua Reynolds, notable among which was Reynold's portrait of Colonel (later General) Tarleton, a Liverpool celebrity, who became a Tory Member of Parliament for Liverpool and a political opponent of Roscoe. Thomas Taylor, a local businessman and amateur art dealer, spoke of the 1784 exhibition as 'as good as the Royal Academy' and the Tarleton portrait as 'proving as hot as fire'.[28] C.P. Darcy describes the exhibition as 'a shrewd blending of London and provincial talent, which please patrons and public'.[29] A further exhibition was held in 1787, the last for a period of twenty-four years. Roscoe's brother-in-law, Daniel Daulby, who with Roscoe and others were active members of the society which pioneered these exhibition, explained the reasons for their suspension.

'The Society is again dormant, not for want of subscribers to support it. The subscriptions would be ample, the assistants and students would be sufficiently numerous to carry it on, and a triennial Exhibition would again be honoured with the works of the first painters. The two last have increased the taste of the town for the arts, and many excellent paintings which were sent to the Exhibition without any particularly interested view, but merely

---

26 See Preface to the catalogue of the Roscoe Collection of Pictures, deposited by the Trustees of the Liverpool Institution in the Walker Art Gallery, Liverpool, written by Maurice W. Bracknell.

27 William Roscoe, a Memoir by Godfrey W. Matthews, pp.17 and 18 and Joseph Mayer, Early Exhibitions of Art in Liverpool, 1876.

28 W Barnard Faraday, Memoirs and Proceedings of the Manchester Literary and Philosophical Society, XLIV (1900) page 38.

29 C.P. Darcy, Encouragement of the Fine Arts in Lancashire, Manchester 1976 p.31.

to promote a general taste for the arts, have been purchased and remain in the town. It is, however, much to be regretted that in a mercantile town like Liverpool, it is extremely difficult to meet with gentlemen who have leisure to conduct such a society; to the want of such gentlemen may be attributed the present suspension of the society for the promotion of the arts.'[30]

The early years of the 19th century brought about a tremendous surge in commercial prosperity in Liverpool, accompanied by an increase in civic pride and the construction of classical buildings and monuments as well as by a renewed interest in the arts. The Liverpool Academy was revived in 1810 by artists and civic leaders and exhibitions were held every year from 1810 to 1815. The Liverpool Royal Institution, a foundation devoted to the spread of learning, was inaugurated in 1817 and took the Liverpool Academy under its wing, providing accommodation for study, workshops, exhibitions and a permanent art collection. Roscoe was the pioneer of all this activity as a young man of twenty: he had the satisfaction of seeing in his later years the seed he had sown bear much fruit.

In 1774 Roscoe completed his articles and was admitted an attorney of the Court of the King's Bench. He entered into partnership with a firm which came to be known as Aspinall, Roscoe and Lace. It was at this time that Roscoe became a welcome guest at the home of William Griffies, a linen draper in Castle Street.[31] His second daughter, Jane, shared many of his literary interests and they became the closest of friends.[32] At that stage in her life, Jane kept a diary with a daily record of events. Roscoe thought it would be a good idea if, in place of the diary, they could both enter into regular correspondence, despite the fact that they both lived in the same town. He wrote, 'Nothing could be more innocent - nothing more rational: and though the generality of mankind might think it a little silly, I hope you and I have too great an opinion of our own consequence, to be guided by vulgar opinions'.[33]

---

30 J.A. Picton, Memorials of Liverpool (London 1875), p.211, quotation from a letter to John Holt.

34 Liverpool Directories 1774, 1777 and 1781.

32 Roscoeana - F.W. Dunston pp.69, 118 and 121. Jane was the great-grand daughter of Joshua Ambrose, M.A., who was educated at Harvard College, New England from 1650 to 1653 and completed his studies at Oxford, before becoming Minister of West Derby Chapel in 1665 and Vicar of Childwall. The Ambrose family, many of them clergy, came from Ormskirk and appear to have been proteges of the Earl of Derby.

33 Life of W.R. Vol.1, p.45.

And so a correspondence began which continued for many years until their marriage. Their correspondence throws a good deal of light on their character. Roscoe's letters reflect his changing moods before and during their engagement - sometimes insufferably pompous, sometimes gloomy, sometimes full of fun and sometimes tender and romantic in the extreme. To encourage Jane to keep on writing and because so much time and ink were being consumed in this correspondence, Roscoe decided to present her with a fancy inkstand. He knew already what her reaction would be and expressed his thoughts in verse:-[34]

> 'A present I've bought for my fair,
> An inkstand of curious device,
> But to tell what it cost I'll forbear,
> She'll say 'twas a barbarous price.
> For he ne'er could be true, she averr'd,
> Who in nicknacks his money would spend,
> And I lov'd her the more when I heard
> Such savingness at her tongue's end.'

Throughout their long and happy married life Roscoe was the spendthrift partner, whilst Jane struggled to curb his extravagance. Roscoe's early romantic poems, addressed to Jane under the poetic name of 'Julia', are amongst his liveliest and best.

Roscoe worked for three years in the partnership before becoming engaged to be married to Jane and a further four years before he felt himself to be sufficiently established in his profession to marry in 1781. During these years he laboured indefatigably and as the years passed found time to engage increasingly in political and literary activities. He was also able, by judicious and careful buying, to build up his library and to form his collection of ancient manuscripts, prints and works of art.[35] Three years before their marriage Jane, on a visit to London, offered to help find books suitable for his collection. However the prices were well beyond their means. Jane was the first of many to search for treasures on Roscoe's behalf.

---

34 Life of W.R. Vol.1, p.50.
35 Life of W.R. Vol.1, p.51.

William Roscoe and Jane Griffies were married by license at the Chapel of St. Anne, Liverpool, on February 22, 1781.[36] They enjoyed forty years of happy married life and were proud of their large and united family. Of their seven sons one became a banker, one a merchant, two of them lawyers, one a doctor and one an author. Many of their family were as prolific in their writing and as varied in their interests as their parents. One of Roscoe's numerous grand-children, Sir Henry Roscoe, F.R.S., was an eminent scientist and became Professor of Chemistry at Manchester University. Once Roscoe attempted to research his own family history, but achieving little success in his enquiries, he told a genealogist friend that he was proud to think of himself 'as a good patriarch and the proper person to begin a family'.[37] Roscoe's sister Margaret and her husband, Daniel Daulby, and their family lived at Birchfield, Folly Lane, Liverpool and later at Rydal Mount in Westmorland. Daniel, the author of A Descriptive Catalogue of the Works of Rembrandt, 1796, had much in common with his brother-in-law, sharing many of the same interests.[38] As members of the Liverpool Academy, they were deeply involved in the promotion of art education; also they collaborated in the campaign for the abolition of the slave trade.

In the early years of his married life, Roscoe became increasingly interested in Italian literature, art and culture. His interest was further stimulated by a chance meeting with Henry Fuseli, a Swiss born artist, on a business visit to London in 1782.[39] Fuseli's drawings from Lear and Macbeth had made a deep impression on the British Ambassador in Berlin in 1765 - so much so that he persuaded Fuseli to move to London, where Sir Joshua Reynolds encouraged him to take up painting. Fuseli spent

---

36 William Roscoe, A Memoir by G.W. Mathews p.16. The Chapel of St. Anne was built in 1772 at the expense of Thomas Dobb, a cabinet-maker, his brother Richard, and Henry North, a fruit merchant. It stood on a site at the Everton end of St. Anne's Street and had the most fashionable congregation in the town. Pews were sold for sixty to seventy guineas and there were no free seats! The neighbourhood deteriorated by the mid-nineteenth century and the chapel, which had fallen into disrepair was demolished in 1871. Gore's Directory of Liverpool and the Annals of Liverpool.

37 Life of W.R. Vol.1, p.4.

38 C.P. Darcy - The Encouragement of the Fine Arts in Lancashire 1760 to 1860, p.137. Manchester, 1976 'Daniel Daulby was a patron and close friend of Joseph Wright of Derby in the artist's last years. This lawyer and banker, a man of considerable culture,brought together in the late eighteenth century a large collection of books, prints and drawings and an interesting selection of Old Masters and contemporary artists.

39 Life of W.R. Vol.1, p.65.

eight years in Italy (1770 to 1778) studying Michelangelo before returning to England. Roscoe and Fuseli, as a result of their meeting in 1782, became life-long friends and kept up a correspondence for nearly forty years, supporting and encouraging one another. Roscoe delivered a course of lectures in 1785 on 'The History of Art' and on the 'Knowledge and use of Prints and the History and Progress of the Art of Engraving'. In these lectures he commended the work of Fuseli to the people of Liverpool.[40] Roscoe's correspondence with Fuseli is mainly on matters relating to the arts, and records many examples of his patronage of Fuseli, who was often in financial difficulties.[41]

It was at the time of Fuseli's first visit to Liverpool in 1785 that Roscoe wrote a long poem entitled 'The Art of Engraving', which is remarkable for several reasons. His son, Henry, drew attention to 'the intimate acquaintance with the different styles of the great masters in the branch of art' displayed by his father in this poem.[42] It is also remarkable because of the reference to 'the Great Lorenzo' and his part in the revival of art in fifteenth century Florence,[43] and the writing of whose biography was to engage Roscoe's leisure hours for several years. Roscoe introduced his illustrious hero by adding to the poem a concise and revealing foot-note:

'Lorenzo de'Medici, called the Magnificent, (born in 1448, died in 1492) was the director of the Florentine republic for upwards of twenty years, and the father of John de'Medici, afterwards pope, by the name of Leo X. To the munificence and taste of Lorenzo is principally to be attributed the sudden progress of the fine arts in Italy at the close of the fifteenth century. But this is only a small part of his praise. If a full enquiry be made into his life and character, he will appear to be not only one of the most extraordinary, but, perhaps, upon the whole, the most, extraordinary man that any age or nation produced.'

It appears that the more Roscoe learnt from his intensive study of the great Lorenzo, the more he began to see himself cast in the role of a latter-day Lorenzo, patron of the arts, merchant prince and benefactor, doing for Liverpool what Lorenzo did for Florence over three hundred years earlier. In cherishing this ambition, Roscoe showed no trace of

---

40 Life of W.R. Vol.1, p.66.

41 Roscoe Papers Nos. 714 and 1593.

42 Life of W.R. Volume 1, pp.66,67.

43 See Roscoe's poem, 'In Elder Greece' in Chandler's William Roscoe of Liverpool, p.448.

arrogance. Washington Irving, the American man of letters, in an essay on Roscoe, wrote - "Like his own Lorenzo de'Medici, on whom he seems to have fixed his eye, as on a pure model of antiquity, he has interwoven his life with the history of his native town, and has made the foundations of its fame the monuments of his virtues."[44]

Roscoe's interest in Italy stemmed back to his early days as a solicitor's clerk. Francis Holden, a young school-master, shared his enthusiasm for Latin and Italian literature with Roscoe and a few friends, helping them with the study of the two languages. On long walks together Holden would recite his favourite Italian poems to his admiring and perhaps envious companions.[45] Roscoe became deeply interested in the period of Italian history extending from the late 15th century until the mid 16th century. He formed the opinion that 'almost all the great events, from which Europe derives its present advantages, are to be traced to those times'.[46] He was astonished and delighted to find that this was a time 'when Venice, Milan, Rome, Florence, Bologna, Ferrara ... vied with each other not in arms but in science and in genius, and the splendour of a court was estimated by the number of learned men who illustrated it by their presence ...'.

Roscoe's decision to write a biography of Lorenzo may not have taken his friends by surprise. He left no stone unturned in his search for sources of information regarding Lorenzo in England. He read everything relevant he could lay hands on, though unfortunately there was no public library in Liverpool at that time. He searched bookshops in London and was fortunate enough to buy books, presumably through an agent, at the sale of the Crevenna library in Amsterdam and of the Pinelli library in London, both of which took place shortly before he embarked on his project. At these sales he was able to procure a number of scarce and valuable works, for which he had hitherto enquired in vain.[47]

Some of the books he required and virtually all the documents, likely to be helpful, could only be found in Italy. His business commitments ruled out all possibility of going to Italy himself. He was not adventurous and

---

44 Washington Irving, The Sketch Book (Essay on Roscoe 1819-1820) p.24.

45 Life of W.R. Vol.1, p.21.

46 William Roscoe, Life of Lorenzo - Preface - page 7 et seq.

47 Life of Lorenzo (Bohn edition) p.518 note 183 - Roscoe states that 'a considerable collection of the ancient editions of the 'Rappresentazione' of the fifteenth century, formerly in the Pinelli library had fallen into my hands'. Further details regarding the principal sources used by Roscoe in his 'Life of Lorenzo' may be found in the chapter on Roscoe's writings.

strangely enough never expressed any desire to travel abroad. Even journeys to London he found irksome and never really felt at ease except in or near his native town. Providentially, William Clarke, the son of a Liverpool banker and a companion in his early studies, was advised by his doctor to spend the winter of 1789 in a warmer climate.[48] He rented a villa at Fiesole, only three miles above Florence. On hearing of this, Roscoe invited him to assist him with his own project. Clarke welcomed the invitation and nobody could have been more enthusiastic or better qualified to gather the resource-material Roscoe needed. The Grand Duke readily allowed free access to his palaces, galleries, museums and libraries to all bona fide scholars - a privilege only secured by means of bribery in other Italian cities. Even the state archives lodged at the Palazzo Vecchio were made accessible. The Grand Duke's librarian, Canonico Bandini and the Abate Fontani, keeper of the Riccardi Library, were equally helpful.

Clarke also obtained a copy of 'The Life of Lorenzo' by Fabroni, an Italian scholar, published in 1784. He read it with great care, taking special note of the authorities used. Shortly before his return to England, in a letter to Roscoe dated March 1790, he wrote - 'In a few days I remove to Florence to remain there from fifteen to twenty days, totally occupied with your hero, who has won my warmest veneration. I have gone through Fabroni's work. Many of his authorities will be useful to you. The life which is composed in Latin, with laboured attention to style, has more regard to the public conduct of Lorenzo than to his private character ... Yours, I am convinced, will be a more entertaining work.'[49] Clarke having completed his labours, on his return to Liverpool, handed over to Roscoe the fruits of his research, enabling him to proceed with his magnum opus, which took six years to complete and publish. Roscoe soon discovered that he had undertaken a far more arduous and complicated task than he had anticipated and the chief obstacle to quick progress was the pressure of his exacting business.

The publication of the Life of Lorenzo de'Medici in 1796 proved an immediate success, three editions appearing within three years. The biography gave great pleasure to many leading literary figures, among whom was Lord Orford (Horace Walpole), who in a letter to a friend, the

---

48   Life of W.R. Vol.1 Chapter 5, p.147.

49   Life of W.R. Vol. 1, p.150.

Revd. Mark Noble, author of 'Memoirs of the Medici Family', wrote 'Mr Roscoe is, I think, by far the best of our historians, both for beauty and style, and for deep reflections'.[50] Fabroni, by that time Principal of the University of Pisa, was quick to commend Roscoe's biography to Italian readers. He had originally intended to publish an Italian version of his Life of Lorenzo, which had been written in Latin. After reading Roscoe's work he changed his mind and asked the Cavaliero Gaetano Mechevini to make an Italian translation of Roscoe's book.[51] This was published in Pisa under Fabroni's patronage in 1799.

Soon after publication of his 'Life of Lorenzo', Roscoe decided, much to the surprise of his friends, to retire from his practice as a solicitor at the age of forty three years. There is no evidence to suggest that Roscoe, encouraged by the success of the Life of Lorenzo, entertained the idea of making a living by writing books. It was with considerable reluctance that he embarked on his second major literary work, the Life and Pontificate of Leo the Tenth. Certainly the income derived from the 'Life of Lorenzo' was substantial, but by no means sufficient to provide permanently for the needs of the Roscoe family. Hartley Coleridge, referring to Roscoe's early retirement remarked that 'business must have been indeed extensive and lucrative to enable him (Roscoe) to escape from its trammels so soon with a competent fortune and an unspotted reputation'. In the late 18th and early 19th centuries it was by no means impossible for a hardworking lawyer, whether in rapidly expanding Liverpool, Edinburgh or elsewhere in Britain to amass a small fortune within a period of twenty years. From the beginning Roscoe found his work as an attorney distasteful and always felt a longing for the day when 'he would be free to enjoy a few tranquil years of leisure and retirement to pursue his own interests and to be free to avoid crowds, noise and contention in the company of a few chosen friends.[52] One of his close friends, William Rathbone, a wealthy ship-owner engaged principally in the American trade, a Quaker and an outspoken opponent of the slave trade and advocate of free trade, wrote to Roscoe, reproaching him for his early retirement. He received Roscoe's uncompromising reply:- "I am much obliged by the tailpiece to your letter of today, though, to say the truth, it amounts to nothing more than calling

---

50 Life of W.R. Vol.1, p.162.

51 William Roscoe, The Life of Lorenzo de' Medici, London, Bohn Libraries Edition 1898, Memoir of the Author, p.31.

52 Life of W.R. Vol.1, p.203.

William Rathbone of Liverpool, 1757 - 1809, Roscoe's friend.

me (in very friendly terms) an idle and extravagant fellow, who is playing off the artful trick of getting hold of the conveniences and pleasures of life without performing any of its duties. This I relish the worse, as I am not sure that there is not some degree of truth in it; but I am much surer, that to toil and labour for the sake of labouring and toiling, is a much more foolish part; and that it is the curse of God upon avarice, that he who has given himself up too long to its dominion shall never be able to extricate himself from its chains. Surely man is the most foolish of all animals, and civilised man the most foolish of men. Anticipation is his curse; and to prevent the contingency of evil, he makes life itself only one continued evil. Health, wisdom, peace of mind, conscience are all sacrificed to the absurd purpose of heaping up, for the use of life, more than life can employ, under the flimsy pretext of providing for his children, till practice becomes habit, and we labour on till we are obliged to take our departure, as tired of the world as we are unprepared for the rational happiness of the next. I have much more to say to you on this subject, but this is not the place for it. I shall therefore leave you to your:

'Double double

Toil and trouble,

Fire burn, and caldron bubble.'

whilst I go to the arrangement of the fifth class of my plants, and take my chance of a few years in a workhouse, some fifty years hence, which I shall think well compensated by having had the lot to live so long."[53]

Nobody could ever have accused Roscoe of idleness. He expected to find 'rational happiness' in the next world, and for him 'rational happiness' would have meant activity rather than eternal rest. He was open to criticism for extravagance. His impulsive nature made him inclined to take risks. In a letter dated December 13th 1796 sent to Roscoe at Birchfield, Rathbone, referring to crates of ware Roscoe was interested in buying, chaffed him for arguing on the folly of toiling for wealth, at the same time, indulging himself with all that wealth can purchase.[54]

A year later in 1797 Roscoe surprised his family and friends by his decision to go to London in order to enter Gray's Inn, with a view to becoming a barrister. Perhaps he had second thoughts about Rathbone's advice and began to feel that, after all, he was shirking his responsibilities.

---

53 Life of W.R. Vol.1, pp.204-5.

54 Roscoe Papers 3059 - China ware or perhaps glass -

One term of residence proved enough for Roscoe and he wasted no time in returning to Liverpool. There must have been good reason for his decision to withdraw completely from the legal profession, though it is evident that Henry, his son and biographer was disappointed. Apart from anything else Roscoe disliked London. At that time he wrote to his brother-in-law, Daniel Daulby, who had recently moved to the Lake District:-[55]

'From the midst of all the delights that London affords, I condescend to salute the lonely inhabitants of the solitary hills and cheerless wilds of Westmorland. Here everything is life and gaiety; the rattling of wheels, the winding of horns, and the ringing of bells, performing a continual chorus; whilst with you, the chirping of a robin red-breast, or the lowing of a cow, is all that gratifies your ears. At this hour you are, perhaps, complaining of the clear and nipping air, or incommoded with the beams of the noonday sun; whilst here an impenetrable vapour screens us from his rays, and forms a soft and sociable atmosphere, breathed from the lungs of a million people, who would not exchange this happiness for any other the world could give. But to tell you the truth, my dear Dan, I begin to be shockingly tired of my abode.'

The population of Liverpool increased almost tenfold from 20,000 to 195,000 in Roscoe's lifetime.[56] As many, if not more, elegant Georgian houses were built in Liverpool as in any other town in Britain. Although Liverpool was essentially Roscoe's home, he lived in a succession of houses. Philippe Daudy, in his recent book - 'Les Anglais - Portrait of a People'[57] tells us that "an Englishman's house is like any other consumer necessity. Like his wardrobe or his car, it answers the need of a moment. It can grow with his family, improve or deteriorate according to his fortunes." Roscoe may appear typically English in this respect. Once in a letter to his wife, Jane, when away on legal business, he wrote "If I might indulge a wish, it would be retire with you to a peaceful retreat, where with a sparing competence, we might live to ourselves and bid adieu to an employment which preys on my happiness and disgusts me with myself and mankind."[58] He did in fact move in 1790 to what was then an idyllic retreat, the Dingle

---

55 Life of W.R. Vol.1, pp.214 and 215.

56 William Roscoe - by George Murphy, Liverpool, 1981, p.30.

57 'Les Anglais' by Philippe Daudy, 1991, p.3. Daudy compares the English attitude to the French tradition, which is 'to invest the family home (however humble), with all the permanence and the sacred aura of ownership, 'la propriety'.

58 Life of W.R. Vol.1, page 205.

in Toxteth Park, from which he could see the Mersey and the distant Welsh mountains, a sight he had enjoyed as a small child from his first home on Mount Pleasant. This romantic residence inspired him to write poetry, but evidently was less convenient for Jane and the expanding family. Within three years the Roscoes moved again to a more ample, less rickety and more solid home, within the town, Birchfield, Folly Lane, where his sister and family, the Daulbys, had resided before moving to the Lake District. Six years later, three years after Roscoe's retirement from his practice, he felt able to buy a splendid mansion outside the town, Allerton Hall, which provided everything he needed, except that it became necessary to make substantial additions a few years later to accommodate his library and collections.[59] How it was possible for the Roscoes to live comfortably in this establishment on 'a modest competence' is hard to understand. It must have required skilful management on the part of his wife.

Two contemporary poets, of whom Roscoe had formed a high opinion, were Samuel Taylor Coleridge and Robert Burns, both of whom he had hoped to welcome at Liverpool. Roscoe thought so highly of Burns that he took the opportunity of paying him a compliment in his life of Lorenzo.[60] Roscoe found himself thinking of Burns, when describing Lorenzo's use of country dialect in a poem entitled 'La Nencia da Barberino'. He drew the attention of his readers 'to the beautiful and interesting poems of the Ayrshire ploughman' and ventured to assert 'that neither in Italy, nor in any other country has this species of poetry been cultivated with greater success. The Cotter's Saturday Night is perhaps, unrivalled of its kind in any language.'[61] Both Burns and Roscoe incurred unpopularity because of their sympathy with the ideals which inspired the French Revolution in its early stages. Both were equally disillusioned by the atrocities which accompanied the revolution and by the military dictatorship which emerged. Burns notified Roscoe of his intention to come to Liverpool, but the visit never took place owing to Burns's untimely death in 1796. After the death of Burns, Roscoe was sent a manuscript of his own poem, 'Song for the Anniversary of the French Revolution - O'er the vine-covered hills and gay regions of France' - copied by Burns in his own handwriting with an

---

59 G.W. Mathews, Memoir of Wm. Roscoe, 1931, page 8 - 'Roscoe's father is said to have been butler at Allerton Hall before becoming an innkeeper.

60 Life of W.R. Vol.1, page 233.

61 William Roscoe, Life of Lorenzo de Medici, page 200 (Bohn Edition) and page 517 note 176.

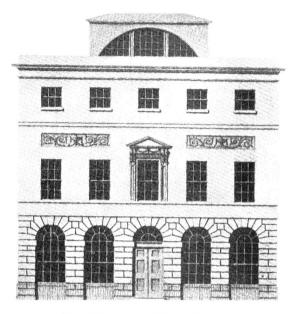

The Athenaeum, Church Street,
which Roscoe helped to found in 1798.

The Botanic Garden, Liverpool,
Roscoe delivered the opening address in 1802.

accompanying note - 'the enclosed poem, found among Burns's manuscripts might be acceptable to you amongst your own, from the circumstances of its being written in the poor bard's hand two years ago, and was given by him to myself, as a poetical production to which he was enthusiastically partial.'[62] Roscoe was scandalised by what he considered to have been the outrageous treatment of Scotland's national poet by his own people. In writing to Mr Edwards, a clergyman in Birmingham, he said:- "His (Burns') example has fixed the value of high poetical attainments in Scotland, and they amount to the place of an exciseman, with a salary of £50 per annum. Such has been the munificence of the Scotch peerage and the Scotch gentry to a man who has done more honour to his country than all the throat-cutters it ever bred.[63] May they never have another opportunity of insulting genius with paltry and insidious rewards." Dr Currie, a friend and associate of Roscoe in many concerns, literary and political, took the view that Roscoe in his 'Ode on the death of Burns', attacked the ingratitude of Burns' countrymen too violently. Roscoe refused to alter or retract a word of what he had written. Dr. Currie, encouraged by Roscoe, was the author of a 'Life of Burns' written soon after Burns' death.[64]

It was at this time that an institution was founded which still survives and is approaching its bicentenary, namely the Liverpool Athenaeum. Roscoe was an active member and played an important part in the selection and arrangement of books for the library.[65]

One of the attractions of Allerton Hall was that it provided the opportunity for Roscoe to pursue his interest in botany. His interest was practical as well as academic and he was able to collect and cultivate rare plants from abroad, with the help of traders from America, the West Indies and the East. Soon after moving to Allerton, Roscoe played a leading part in establishing the Liverpool Botanical Garden. He delivered an address at the opening ceremony in 1802. Among early visitors to Allerton was Dr Smith, who dedicated his book 'Exotic Botany' to Roscoe.

---

62 Life of W.R. Vol.1, page 233, Letter written by Mrs. Riddell to Roscoe.

63 Life of W.R. Vol 1, p.234.

64 W.W. Currie, Life of Dr. Currie, Vol.1, p.271.

65 Life of W.R. Vol.1, p.230 - see also footnote - Resolution re services of W.R. passed at the Liverpool Athenaeum A.G.M. July 12, 1831.

Any hopes of a life of unbroken leisure in his new home at Allerton were dashed within a year of Roscoe's taking up residence. The family of his friend William Clarke, who had procured in Italy the material for Roscoe's 'Life of Lorenzo' owned a bank in Liverpool, which at the end of 1799 ran into difficulties.[66] Roscoe was invited by the partners to investigate the firm's affairs as legal adviser. This he felt obliged to do and he proved so successful in solving the bank's problems that he was invited to become a partner. It appears that Roscoe was virtually forced against his better judgement to accept the invitation.[67] Hartley Coleridge, writing about Roscoe in 1836 tells us that 'Sir Benjamin Hammet, a London banker, who is said to have held acceptances on the Liverpool Bank to the amount of £200,000, was so struck with Roscoe's abilities in arranging the affairs of the bank, that he pressed him to become a partner in the concern, and that on Roscoe's refusal, he threatened to make it bankrupt and that it was to save his friends that Roscoe yielded. The alteration of his course redounded to his honour, for it arose neither from restlessness, infirmity of purpose, avarice nor ambition, but was a sacrifice of his own leisure and wishes for the benefit of his friends'. This contradicts Edward Morris' suggestion that Roscoe continued to work as a banker in order to earn sufficient money to maintain and educate his large family.[68] Roscoe was to sacrifice his future to save his friends. Under Roscoe's leadership confidence was restored in the bank for a number of years until the final collapse in 1816.

Such was the success of Roscoe's 'Life of Lorenzo' that he was persuaded by a number of admirers to follow it up with a biography of Lorenzo's son, Pope Leo X. Once again he was able to find volunteers willing to collect information in Italy and to carry out research on his behalf. Roscoe found the preparation of this book much more of an undertaking than he had anticipated and his labours were interrupted by his other commitments and by ill-health. However this four volume biography was published in 1805 much to his relief. This work received a mixed reception. It aroused the anger of Catholics and Protestants, some of whose assessment of the book was influenced by religious prejudice rather than unbiased critical analysis. The biography was translated into Italian, French and German and was widely circulated.

---

66   William Roscoe, Life of Lorenzo, Memoir of the Author pp.32-33.

67   Hartley Coleridge, Worthies of Yorkshire and Lancashire, 1836, pp.518, 519.

68   Edward Morris, Riches into Art, Liverpool University Press, Liverpool Historical Essays, p.18.

Although Roscoe became increasingly involved in political activity, he does not appear to have entertained any idea of standing for parliament. The invitation in 1806 by a number of influential citizens, including two of the leading African slave traders of the town, to come forward as a candidate seems to have taken him by surprise.[69] He accepted the challenge and, standing as an independent candidate, was commended to the electorate by his supporters on the grounds of his attachment to liberal principles, his long connection with the town, his fame as a scholar and writer and the universal respect for his personal character. Surprisingly, abolition of the slave trade was hardly mentioned at all during the whole campaign.[70] Everyone knew that Roscoe was the acknowledged leader of the Liverpool abolitionists.

Well aware theirs was a minority opinion, the abolitionists set about their task with determination, but always avoided open and unnecessary provocation. Hence the silence during the campaign. The election was exceptionally long and keenly contested as well as riotous. The Tory candidate, Sir Bannister Tarleton, who was a favourite among those who worked in the Liverpool market, organised a gang known as 'the Butchers', whom Roscoe accused 'of interfering with the conduct of the poll by blocking the way to the hustings to his supporters'. When on the third day 'the Butchers' appeared dressed up as soldiers, a brawl ensued, but Roscoe's supporters managed to chase them away.[71]

One of Roscoe's active supporters in his campaign was the Rev. William Shepherd, born in Liverpool, educated at the Dissenters' Academies at Daventry and Hackney,[72] who returned to his home town as tutor to the children of the Rev. John Yates, minister of the Paradise Street Chapel. In 1791 Shepherd, at the early age of twenty-three, became minister of the Gateacre Unitarian chapel. Shepherd was invited to become a member of the Literary Society formed by Roscoe, which met fortnightly in the homes of its members, who included John Yates, Dr. Currie, William

---

69   Life of W.R. Vol.1, p.353.

70   F.E. Sanderson, Liverpool Abolitionists, Transactions of the Historic Society of Lancashire and Cheshire, 1973, p.223.

71   F.E. Sanderson, The Structure of Politics in Liverpool, 1780-1807, 'Transactions of the Historic Society of Lancashire and Cheshire', 1973, p.78.

72   Roy Porter, English Society in the Eighteenth Century, p.164. The Hackney Academy was described by Burke as 'the new arsenal in which subversive doctrines were forged'. Prestige academies such as Hackney and Warrington and Hoxton were forced to close when church elders could no longer stomach doctrinal anarchy.

Rathbone and others. The society concerned itself with topics of literary, artistic and historical interest, but because some of its members were known to be ardent supporters of reform, having demonstrated a measure of sympathy with the ideals which lay behind the French Revolution at least in its early stages, the society was compelled to suspend its meetings after the Proclamation Against Seditious Meetings issued by the Prime Minister, William Pitt.

Shepherd took a keen interest in Roscoe's preparation for writing his Life of Lorenzo and helped him sift and classify the materials, manuscripts and books, which William Clarke had collected in Florence and sent to Liverpool. Fired with enthusiasm for the achievements of 15th Century Florence, Shepherd decided to write a Life of Poggio Bracciolini, private secretary to eight successive popes, who was made Chancellor of Florence in 1453.[73] Poggio Bracciolini recovered many lost works of Roman literature, collected and restored many treasures of the ancient world and has been aptly described as 'a pioneer of conservation'.[74]

In the 1806 parliamentary election Roscoe proved the most popular candidate. Large sums of money were spent to ensure the success of his campaign[75] and there was talk of prodigious bribery. William Shepherd expressed the opinion that superior organisation and the dedication of his canvassers won the day. Once elected Roscoe, after speaking of his ardent desire for an honourable peace with France, did mention the slave trade, asserting that as the slave trade had been sanctioned by parliament, the latter should give full compensation to all who were to suffer financial loss in the event of abolition. He also briefly outlined his plans for parliamentary reform, many of which were incorporated in the Reform Bill passed under Lord Grey twenty-six years later.

The privilege of representing Liverpool in the debate preceding the passing of the Bill for the Abolition of Slavery gave Roscoe immense satisfaction. He concluded his speech in the House of Commons with these words - "I have long resided in the town of Liverpool; for thirty

---

73 William Shepherd's 'Life of Poggio Bracciolini' was published in London in1802, a second edition appearing in 1837.

74 Graham Murphy, William Roscoe, His Early Ideals and Influence, 1981. Murphy tells us that 'The men, whom Roscoe and Shepherd admired, were model citizens of an ideal city'.

75 F.E. Sanderson, Liverpool and the Slave Trade, Transactions of the Historic Society of Lancashire and Cheshire, 1973 Vol.124, page 165.

William Shepherd, Engraving from the Athenaeum Library.

years I have never ceased to condemn this inhuman traffic; and I consider it the greatest happiness of my existence to lift up my voice on this occasion against it, with the friends of justice and humanity."[76] Soon afterwards, the inaugural meeting of the African Institute, which Roscoe had helped to establish, was held in London. The chairman, was the Duke of Gloucester. At this meeting Wilberforce speaking of Roscoe said:- "Here is a man, who by strength of character has risen above the deep-seated prejudices of his townspeople and eventually won their respect. His future is secure." Roscoe was buoyed up by this false expectation and took little notice of his friend William Rathbone's warning "that knives were being sharpened; that he would not find things easy when he returned". Roscoe failed to take into account the likely reaction in Liverpool to the collapse of the slave trade. Also Roscoe's last speech in parliament was strongly in favour of Catholic emancipation and was certain to have provoked the considerable anti-Catholic element in the town.

After the Passing of the Bill for the Abolition of Slavery in 1806 George III dismissed the coalition 'Ministry of All Talents' led by Lord Grenville,[77] because the cabinet proposed to admit Roman Catholic officers into the British Army and refused to make the promise the King demanded of them never again to raise the matter of Catholic relief in any form. This led to an early dissolution of Parliament in May 1807 and to another general election.

Roscoe returned to his constituency jubilant at the triumphant manner in which the Bill of Abolition had been carried through both Houses of Parliament. In Liverpool he received a rude awakening. Many of his friends and supporters, mounted and on foot, met him in the outskirts of the town. What might have been a triumphal entry soon became a riot, when Roscoe was waylaid by gangs of disgruntled and unemployed seamen armed with cudgels, determined to obstruct the procession.[78] There were violent scenes in the town centre. A number of people were injured, though not seriously, and a horse was stabbed with a knife. Were it not for the forbearance displayed towards the demonstrators by Roscoe's supporters, the consequences might have been much more serious. Roscoe had intended to address the crowds

---

76   F.E. Sanderson, Liverpool Abolitionists. p.223 et seq.

77   G.M. Trevelyan - British History in the Nineteenth Century (1922), pp.116 and 117.

78   Life of W.R. Vol.1, p.392 et seq.

outside his bank, Clarke's and Roscoe's Bank, at the corner of Dale Street and Castle Street, but was persuaded not to attempt it.

His friends, assuring him that the great body of the electors were still favourably disposed towards him, urged him to seek re-election. His son, Henry, tells us that 'his father saw in the exasperation displayed upon his entrance, a determination to decide the contest by tumult and violence; and he did not feel it consistent with his feelings and principles to take any part in transactions which must in all probability have ended in bloodshed.[79] He also tells us there were motives of a different kind which induced him to retire from a second contest. His experience of political life he had found distasteful; the burden of public duties had interfered with the performance of his private duties and an opportunity now offered itself of retiring with honour from a contest, into which his sense of duty, rather than his inclinations, had led him to enter.

Had Roscoe become an M.P. at an earlier stage in his life, he might well have been better able to cope with the rough and tumble of party politics. In the early weeks of his parliamentary career he felt ill at ease. At the age of fifty-three he was very conscious of the fact that he was older than the majority of his colleagues. His impression was that 'the predominating idea of men of all parties is individual, personal aggrandisement and that the welfare of the country is only a secondary consideration.' When in London he missed his wife's presence and support. He was weighed down by a feeling that he must on no account disappoint his constituents. He received a good deal of practical advice before making his big speech in the Abolition debate, first from his friend in Liverpool, the Rev. Dr. William Shepherd, and at the last moment by the Speaker of the House of Commons, who drew him aside and told him exactly where to stand and how to project his voice.[80] Although Roscoe had delivered many learned orations to sympathetic audiences on former occasions in his own town, it may well be that he lacked the rhetorical gifts to impress a highly sophisticated house.

In a number of letters to friends, Roscoe explained his feelings after his decision not to stand again for parliament. Writing to William Smith, M.P. for Norwich on May 11th 1807 he said 'The abuse poured out against me was unbounded. I am represented as an enemy to the King, and as having taken bread out of the mouths of the people of Liverpool by abolishing the

---

79   Life of W.R. Vol.1, p.394. et seq.

80   Life of W.R. Vol.1, Ch.9, p.410.

Slave Trade.[81] Again on May 18th he wrote, 'The torrent of ribaldry and scurrility which has been poured out on me not only viva voce, but from the press, is sufficient to disgust any person with a Liverpool Election ...'

Roscoe's last word on the subject is found in another letter written a month later to his botanist friend, Sir James Smith:-[82]

'in truth my dear friend, it requires but little of the efforts of others to drive me from public life. The only wonder is, that I was ever brought into it; and I sink back with such a rapidity of gravitation into my natural inclination for quiet and retirement, that I totally despair of ever being roused again to a similar exertion. Add to this that the one great object, which was continually before my eyes is now attained, and I shall have the perpetual gratification of thinking that I gave my vote in the assembly of the nation for abolishing the slave trade to Africa. Though not insensible to the state of the country, yet I see no question of equal magnitude; and am fully aware how little my effort could avail in the political struggles of the times. Come then, my friend, and let us again open the book of nature and wander through the fields of Science.'

Despite the trauma of his brief parliamentary career, Roscoe was always ready 'to open the book of nature', and this he did in a highly imaginative way for children and the young in heart. Invited out to dinner one evening in 1806 - to placate his young son, Robert, who wanted to go too - he composed a nursery ballad of junketing when:

> "The children of Earth and the Tenants of Air
>
> For an Evening Amusement together repair."

The ballad was published under the title 'The Butterfly's Ball and the Grasshopper's Feast'.[83] Roscoe set a trend in children's picture books and 40,000 copies were sold in the year of publication, 1807. This has been the most enduring of all Roscoe's writings, though his son, Henry, in the biography of his father, never even mentioned it. A new illustrated

---

81   D.G. Weinglass, Chronological Sketch of Life of Roscoe from The Publishing History of Roscoe's Edition of the Works of Alexander Pope, page 118 at Record Office, Liverpool. Roscoe's original letters are kept at Duke University Library, USA.

82   Roscoe to Sir James Smith, Duke University, USA 377-378, Correspondence.

83   Roscoe Papers 4431 and 4432. Correspondence with Sir George Smart, May 20, 1826. 'The Butterfly's Ball and the Grasshopper's Feast' attracted the attention of George III and the Queen and was set to music at their request by Sir George Smart for the young Princesses Elizabeth, Augusta and Mary. Sir George Smart was Director of Music for the coronations of William IV and Queen Victoria, a distinguished composer and organist.

version came out as recently as 1973 published jointly by Jonathan Cape and the Times.[84]

Although Roscoe's parliamentary career was brief, his interest in politics was life-long. His close association with prominent statesmen and the pamphlets he published on matters of national concern had considerable influence. His pen proved a more powerful instrument for reform than his rhetoric. Roscoe's pamphlets fall broadly into three categories. His chief concern in the early years of the nineteenth century was the war between Great Britain and France. In 1811 he turned his attention to Parliamentary reform and from 1819 he withdrew from political controversy and devoted his energies to broader humanitarian and moral questions such as penal reform and the reformation of criminals. Copies of his more important pamphlets, listed in the appendix of this book are to be found in the Liverpool Record Office.

Roscoe did not hesitate to promote his unpopular views on the Napoleonic War, knowing that in doing so he was in danger of provoking violent opposition. During the Napoleonic Wars Liverpool was well known to have 'displayed an ardour and a greatness of exertion which placed her among the foremost of those who have stood forth to defend their country, their liberties and their independence'.[85]

Roscoe's patriotism was beyond question, but he was as critical of his own country as of any other. He was convinced that it ought to be possible for two powerful nations to live alongside each other in peace. In his opinion, as the war dragged on, not enough effort was being made to secure peace. Nothing infuriated Roscoe more than Canning's suggestion that 'the warfare in which we are engaged was a visitation from heaven' and 'that it was in vain to struggle against the divine wrath'. Roscoe in one of his anti-war pamphlets, speaking of Canning wrote 'Is it not an insult upon common sense to tell us that we can no more prevent the continuance of the war than we can prevent the effects of an earthquake or tornado?'.[86] Roscoe's chief objection to war was that it was an offence against reason. As a humanist and an idealist he firmly believed the madness of war could be avoided. Hartley Coleridge's comments on Roscoe's pamphlets on the war are illuminating:- 'Peace was an object so dear to

---

84   The Times, September 26, 1973.

85   George Chandler, William Roscoe of Liverpool, p.XVI.

86   Life pf W.R. Vol.2, p.41.

Roscoe's heart that he was willing to recommend it by a special pleading; and having persuaded himself that the French ruler really desired peace (which no ruler, legitimate or usurper, whose power is built on military glory can) he thought he was promoting conciliatory dispositions, when endeavouring to convince his inconvincible countrymen, that nothing but their own ill tongues and perverse humours prevented their deadly foe becoming their best and truest friend.'[87]

Roscoe was consistent in his political opinions throughout his life. In 1825 he delivered a paper to the Liverpool Literary and Philosophical Society, which set out the principles for which he stood firmly. In the aftermath of the French Revolution and following the fall of Napoleon, he could see signs of hope:

"Truths hidden to former ages are not only openly asserted, but are diffusing themselves amongst the community with a rapidity which nothing can oppose. Among these may be enumerated the establishment of the great principle of natural and personal rights, with the existence of which a state of slavery is incompatible - the practical refutation of the absurd and dangerous maxim that the safety and wellbeing of a nation depends on the depression and weakness of surrounding states - the open assertion that war is not a necessary evil, but may be averted by means, which it is perfectly in the power of rational beings to adopt - the necessity of a more enlightened jurisprudence, by which the exercise of the benevolent feelings shall be substituted for those of anger, cruelty and revenge and lastly the establishment of the opinion that the rules of morality, which are binding on every individual in private life, are equally applicable to the conduct of governments and the intercourse of nations with each other: these propositions, so various in their objects, so important in their results, are all deducible from one source, and united together in a common origin, being all comprised in the great precept of Christianity, 'to do to others, as we would they should do to us'."[88]

All the things he stood for are clearly indicated in this address:- freedom, human rights, peace and penal reform.

---

87   Hartley Coleridge, Worthies of Lancashire and Yorkshire, 1836 page 72.

88   Life of W.R. Vol.1, p.246.

Soon after retiring from the legal profession and moving into Allerton Hall, Roscoe became not only a reluctant banker, but an enthusiastic farmer, personally supervising the lands surrounding his new home. He wrote to Fuseli, his artist friend and protégé:-[89]

"I consider it as one great secret in the art of living, especially at a time when all the necessaries of life are so high, to obtain subsistence immediately from the earth; and accordingly I am surrounded with cows, hogs, turkeys, geese, cocks, hens and pigeons, which according to the good old maxim, 'Take, Peter, kill and eat', I plunder and slaughter without mercy, and shall be angry with you if you tell me (as is not unlikely) that I am keeping up my paltry existence at the expense of the lives of a number of beings, each of which is ten times happier than myself." What is evident from all this is that Roscoe, with his family and guests, enjoyed home-grown and home-produced food and also that he had friends who took a delight in pulling his leg. Another friend, who never missed an opportunity to tease Roscoe, was William Clarke, who had made possible the writing of his Life of Lorenzo. In 1783 he wrote to congratulate Roscoe on the arrival of yet another child: 'I congratulate you on the increase of your family, but regret the imposition it lays upon you to join in the general contention for wealth!'[90] Clarke took a great interest in the welfare of Roscoe's wife, Jane, and the family. In a letter, dated February 1790, shortly before his return to England from Florence he wrote to Roscoe, 'My truest regards wait on your much esteemed Consorte- you have made a tolerable progress towards filling your Quiver with those young plants which the Prophet or Psalmist David says consist the strength of a house.' Adieu, Le Clerc.[91]

Roscoe became a keen member of the West Derby Agricultural Society and delivered learned lectures on such technical matters as farm leases and relationships between landlord and tenants. He also made a point of reminding the Society and its members of the need to introduce new and improved modes of cultivation suitable to the district.[92] He was not without experience in this field. In 1792 he and Thomas Wakefield, a sugar refiner,

---

89 Life of W.R. Vol.1, p.241 et seq.

90 Roscoe Papers, Letters from Clarke to Roscoe,1783, Record Office, Liverpool Central Library.

91 Roscoe Papers 833, Letter Clarke to Roscoe, 1790.

92 Life of W.R. Vol.2, p.73.

Roscoe's wife, Jane and one of the family
from the painting by John Williamson
in the Roscoe Collection, Walker Art Gallery Liverpool.

engaged together in an experiment, the object of which was to reclaim for agricultural purposes a large tract of land on Chat Moss and Trafford Moss, between Liverpool and Manchester.[93] The rapidly increasing population of Liverpool and Manchester ensured a growing demand for market produce. Roscoe never forgot his father's popular potatoes sold 'at very advanced prices'. Roscoe supervised the work at Chat Moss from its inception, the object being to make the moss land capable of producing a rotation of the best crops. Jeremy Purseglove, in his recent book, The Taming of the Flood, in a section on 18th century 'improvements', describes the work undertaken by Roscoe:- [94] "In 1793 Roscoe began work on Trafford Moss, part of the mighty Chat Moss, 2,500 acres of sphagnum, sundew and bog asphodel. Roscoe's ambition was to drain the whole wetland, and to this end he organised ditching, marling and importation from nearby Manchester of boatload upon boatload of human ordure, which was forked by hand on the moss. One of Roscoe's ideas was a windmill plough, whose sails would actually churn up the bog." Purseglove goes on to say "Unsurprisingly, in view of such projects, he was financially ruined." In fact the Chat Moss experiment was the only project of this nature that Roscoe engaged in and it was not the chief cause of his eventual bankruptcy. Purseglove is right in telling us that the environmental contradictions (and consequences perhaps) implicit in all these 18th century 'improvements' scarcely occurred to anyone at that time.

It is more than likely that the prospect of success at Chat Moss, together with his wide interest in agriculture, contributed to Roscoe's hasty decision to take early retirement in 1796. His experiments at Chat Moss attracted the attention of Sir John Sinclair of Caithness, President of the Board of Agriculture, who asked to be kept fully informed of developments.[95] Roscoe

---

93 Liverpool Banks and Bankers by John Hughes, 1906, p.61.

94 Jeremy Purseglove - The Taming of the Flood page 60 - O.U.P. 1989 and J. Goodier 'Chat Moss - Its Reclamation, Its Pioneers - in Lectures 1970-71 (Eccles and District History Society 1971).

95 It may be of interest that at the time my Roscoe, great three times grandfather was busy with Chat Moss, the indefatigable Sir John Sinclair called at my Macnaughton great great grandfather's sheep farm on Lochtayside in Perthshire. Casting his eye on the burn, he suggested the building of a mill to provide work for the local people. Before leaving the house Sir John persuaded him 'to make immediate preparation for having a mill set a-going, assuring him he would take the responsibility on himself'. This project led to the establishment of two other woollen industries both of which survive today at Pitlochry and Aberfeldy.

was congratulated 'on his skill and zeal in the cause of agriculture'. In June 1815 Mr McVey of Constable, publishers in Edinburgh, wrote to Roscoe saying that he would welcome an account of the Chat Moss Experiment for the supplement to a new Encyclopedia in preparation.[96] Probably it was in response to this request that later the same year Roscoe published a pamphlet on the Improvement of Chat Moss.

It was as a result of Roscoe's agricultural experiments at Chat Moss that he became acquainted with other landowners, interested in new developments, including Mr. G. Tollett of Betley Hall, Staffordshire and Mr. George Wilbraham of Delamere Lodge, Cheshire.[97] These two gentlemen were anxious to arrange a meeting between Mr. Coke of Holkham in Norfolk and Roscoe. Mr. Coke was not only a progressive land-owner. His house was also full of literary treasures and works of art inherited from his great-uncle, Lord Leicester. Mr. Coke wasted no time in inviting Roscoe to be his guest at Holkham. Roscoe hesitated at first, but was eventually prevailed upon to accept by his botanist friend, Sir James Smith, also a friend of Mr. Coke, who promised to join him at Holkham. In a letter dated September 7th 1812 Sir James wrote[98] "We have been spending ten days at Holkham, and I write now at the earnest desire of Mr. Coke to try to persuade you to come and see him and us. He says you have given him some hopes, but have as yet only disappointed him. Now I can conceive nothing more delightful than spending a fortnight with you under this roof (Holkham), and have promised to do so whenever you come. To contemplate his pictures and statues, to rummage amongst his books, drawings, prints and manuscripts, (where we every day find treasures unknown before) is extremely agreeable, and he kindly entrusts the keys to me in full confidence. I found a case of the earliest printed books, which no-one had examined since the time of his great-uncle, Lord Leicester. Such manuscripts of Dante, drawings of the old Italian masters, treasures of European history - you have no idea! The house is one of the finest in Europe and its riches are inexhaustible. But of all things its owner is the best worth your seeing and knowing".

Roscoe's first visit to Holkham exceeded all expectations. The magnificent library had been collected early in the 18th century, but had never been catalogued or received expert attention. It was in Coke's library

96   Roscoe Papers, Liverpool Record Office, 2788.

97   Life of W.R., Vol.2, pp.78, 79.

98   Life of W.R., Voi.2, p.80.

that Roscoe discovered one of the lost volumes of Leonardo da Vinci's treatises on mechanics.[99] This manuscript volume, by the hand of Leonardo da Vinci himself, was of special interest because he wrote it from right to left, so that it could easily be read with the help of a mirror. The theme of this dissertation was 'on the nature, weight and force of water' and was illustrated by many drawings in the margin by the artist himself. Another book of great interest was a volume of original drawings by Raphaël of architectural remains of ancient Rome, executed at the request of Pope Leo X and referred to by Camolli in his life of the painter and by Roscoe in his life of Leo. Roscoe was also much interested to discover a superb copy of Livy,[100] which had belonged to Alfonso, King of Naples, to whom it had been presented by Cosimo de' Medici. Many of the volumes in the library needed binding and at Roscoe's suggestion were sent to John Jones of Liverpool.[101] The work done by Jones in binding these precious books was of a very high standard. Coke of Holkham wrote, 'a barbarous provincial town was coming to be known by every kind of literary enterprise'.

A year later Mr. Coke and other guests, whom Roscoe met at Holkham, accepted an invitation to stay at Allerton. The hospitality accorded by the Roscoe family was greatly appreciated and much interest was shown in Roscoe's 'enlightened' Liverpool friends. Among the guests was the Rev. Dr. Parr, a clerical don and history tutor from Oxford, who having greatly admired Roscoe's Life of Lorenzo de' Medici, wrote to its author welcoming the book and offering some critical comments.[102] Dr.Parr and Roscoe kept closely in touch for the rest of their lives. Dr. Parr submitted a sermon on 'Patriotism', he had preached in 1803 at the Parish Church at Hatton on the occasion of a Public Fast, the equivalent of a National Day of Prayer.'[103]

Roscoe wrote in reply, 'although I agree with you in your definition of patriotism, and in the inferences you draw from it as to the indispensable duty and necessity of a vigorous and national defence, yet I conceive this is not the only form in which the efforts of a true patriot may be displayed'. Roscoe continued, 'You have well observed that our patriotism must not

99   Sir Alfred Shennan, Introduction to Chandler's William Roscoe of Liverpool, p.XVII.

100   Life of W.R. Vol.2, p.86.

101   John Jones later became librarian of the Liverpool Athenaeum and was succeeded in that position by his son, William Roscoe Jones.

102   Dr Parr's full name was the Revd. Dr. W. Parr Gresswell, but he was always spoken of as Dr Parr by the Roscoe family.

103   Life of W.R. Vol.2, Ch.13.

be confined to the endurance of pain or the surrender of life itself'. He insisted that a true patriot must never regard war as inevitable and must actively work for peace and reconciliation. In days when the 'my country right or wrong' mentality dominated church and society, Roscoe's sentiments were not always welcome.

Miss Aikin, the daughter of Dr. Aikin, a friend of Roscoe, happened to be a guest at Allerton at the time of Roscoe's oldest daughter Mary Ann's birthday.'[104] Egged on by Miss Aikin, Roscoe decided the occasion required:

> 'pomp and feast and revelry
>
> with masque and antique pageantry.'

The family together composed a dramatic poem in the form of a masque, Roscoe himself writing the part of Peace, taken by his youngest daughter, Jane. This was unsophisticated entertainment, but no doubt it was enjoyed by all. Among many visitors to Allerton was Maria Edgeworth, a successful novelist and friend of Sir Walter Scott. Her impressions of Allerton Hall are interesting. Mr Roscoe's Lancashire accent seemed greatly to amuse her.

A considerable amount of family correspondence still survives in the Record Office at Liverpool. Mrs. Jane Roscoe regularly kept in touch with her children when away from home, informing them of family news. Roscoe Paper No. 3714 is a good example of such a letter, in which she writes, "Charles, the pony, has been returned to Speke on account of his bad behaviour... I am going to take the girls to the theatre for Mr. Barrymore's benefit - the play is The Chapter of Accidents. We have found a nice place to bathe at Garston beyond the salt works'. Jane mentions various visitors including Mr. Stock, the son of the Bishop of Kilkenny. 'Mr. Shepherd (The Rev. Dr. William) has brought over a very rare flower, large and more beautiful than the night-blooming Cerus, which Mr. Roscoe has drawn'. Jane also speaks of the melancholy fate of a young family friend, Peter Moss.

On a trip to London with his brother Edward, James wrote to his mother from the Temple Coffee House describing their visit.[105] Both had been much shaken by the journey on the mail coach and they were hoping to get a lift back to Liverpool on a chaise. Public transport was notoriously dangerous in those days as well as uncomfortable. It is no wonder Roscoe had no desire to venture abroad.

---

104   Life of W.R. Vol.2, p.70.

105   Roscoe Papers 3714.

A distinguished sculptor, J. Gibson, (1790 to 1866) described as 'the third star in the Neo-Classical firmament after Canova and Thorwaldsen',[106] was a protégé of Roscoe. Gibson, like Roscoe, was the son of a market gardener. Roscoe was quick to recognise his genius and encouraged him to study in London and Rome, where he became a pupil of Canova. In a letter, dated May 1818, he wrote "I have not forgotten your early attentions to me and which brought me to the notice of friends, whose generosity has opened the gates of Rome to me.[107] Yes, here I am and could be contented for ever in Rome, for I like it more and more ... at present I have in hand the model of a shepherd-boy, sleeping (my own design), which I have been studying from nature". Some years later Gibson presented a bust of Roscoe in marble to the Liverpool Institution. Canova, his teacher, on hearing about Roscoe, suggested he be given 'the hair of Euripides'. Roscoe did not forget that his hero, Lorenzo de' Medici, took a promising sculptor called Michaelangelo under his wing, who in due course moved on from Florence to Rome.

Roscoe himself was a competent painter of flowers and birds. Audubon, the American painter-naturalist, was acquainted with Roscoe and kept him informed of his activities. In a letter to Roscoe in 1826 he said "that his great work is at last under way. How long it will be able to bear itself up is a matter of doubt and concern. It is publishing however here in Edinburgh by Mr. W. Lizars, an eminent artist and man of excellent character and great performance and amiability. I have hopes I will not disappoint my friends or the world at large."[108] The great work referred to is 'The Birds of America, from Original Drawings with 435 Plates showing 1,065 Figures' published in 1827. These paintings are considered to be the most dramatic pictures of birds ever published.

In the latter part of the eighteenth century, when life expectancy was much lower than it is today, many minors, bereft of their parents, became wards of court. As a lawyer Roscoe would have been acutely aware of the need for responsible guardians and took on responsibility for two orphaned families. One family consisted of two girls, boarders at a school near the home of Lady Amelia Hume, a friend of the Roscoes. Lady Hume sent Roscoe a letter reporting on their progress in 1804.

---

106 Oxford Companion to Art, p.476.

107 Life of W.R., Vol 2, p.45.

108 Roscoe Papers.

Roscoe thanked her for sending 'so particular and favourable an account of his young wards and promised to send her some plants from the Botanical Garden without delay.'[109] The Lowndes family consisted of three boys and a girl."[110] One of the boys, William, appears to have been able but indecisive. He matriculated at Oxford in 1811 entering Brasenose College. Dr. Parr was able to keep a fatherly eye on him. Eventually Henry Brougham arranged for William to enter Lincoln's Inn along with Robert Roscoe. In 1827 William Lowndes decided to withdraw his application for a Law Professorship at London University and apply instead for a Professorship of Greek. Roscoe's responsibility for the care and education of his own family of ten children together with at least two orphaned families must have been a heavy burden.

A poor Welsh fisher-lad was always made welcome at Allerton and treated with kindness and respect. His name was Richard Robert Jones.[111] In his fishing boat on the coast of Wales, at the age of twenty, he had learnt Latin, Greek and Hebrew as well as French and Italian. He could translate Latin into English or Welsh with the utmost ease. Richard was a prodigy who combined knowledge of languages, literature and ancient civilisation with a complete lack of common sense and a complete disregard for his appearance and cleanliness, so that he was incapable of work. One evening in the presence of a group consisting of Roscoe and his learned friends, Richard astonished the company with his fluency and knowledge, explaining that he had mastered these languages without the help of a teacher. One day Richard had an interview with the erudite Dr. Parr, the Oxford don, which left the doctor completely out of his depth. Dr. Parr 'rather precipitately retreated, leaving a token of liberality in the hands of the poor scholar'. Asked afterwards what he thought of the learned doctor, Richard replied, 'He is less ignorant than most men'.[112] So great was Roscoe's interest in and concern for this character that he wrote 'A Story of Richard', which was sold to raise money for his upkeep as well as a sonnet in Richard's honour. The booklet was published in London in 1822.

Ironically the end of the Napoleonic Wars in 1815, which Roscoe had so long desired, brought financial ruin to the bank for which he was

---

109   Roscoe Papers 2174.

110   Roscoe Papers Nos. 470, 471, 597,1166,1868, 2459, 2464, 2901, 2904, 2910 for correspondence regarding the Lowndes family.

111   Life of W. R. Vol.2, pp.283, et seq.

112   Life of W.R. Vol. 2, pp 288 et seq.

CLARKES & ROSCOE'S BANK, 1792
Corner of Dale Street and Castle Street

responsible, and to himself. Roscoe faced this tragic reversal of fortune with remarkable equanimity and courage. Sydney Jones, on the occasion of the Roscoe Centenary Exhibition in 1931 said - "Roscoe bore his misfortunes with the same imperturbability and the same calm with which he had borne his wealth."[113]

Before the final collapse, it became evident that the greater part of the property of the partners would have to be sold. Without a murmur of complaint, Roscoe set about the task of preparing catalogues for the sale of his books, paintings, manuscripts and art treasures. On December 18th 1815 Mrs. Roscoe sent a letter to Mrs. Rathbone, adding a post-script - "In the course of the ensuing week, I expect the whole of the books and pictures to be gone and I shall not have the misery of viewing Mr. Roscoe's silent submission to the painful duty of dismissing his constant companions of nearly forty years."[114] The sonnet he wrote on parting with his books is one of the best of his poems:

> As one who destined from his friends to part
>> Regrets his loss, but hopes again erewhile
>> To share their converse and enjoy their smile,
>> And tempers, as he may, affliction's dart;
> Thus loved associates! chiefs of elder art!
>> Teachers of wisdom! who could once beguile
>> My tedious hours and lighten every toil,
> I now resign you; nor with fainting heart -
>> For, pass a few short years, or days, or hours,
>> And happier seasons may their dawn unfold,
>> And all your sacred fellowship restore;
> When, freed from earth, unlimited its powers,
>> Mind shall with mind direct communion hold,
>> And kindred spirits meet - to part no more.[115]

The partners of the bank had invested large sums of money in land

---

113 Centenary Address by C. Sydney Jones delivered at the Library, William Brown Street, Liverpool, 1931.

114 Roscoe Papers 3079.

115 Roscoe Papers 3898 and Life of W.R., Vol.2, p.113.

(Chat Moss), coal mines and property, which they were obliged to sell at a substantial loss. Roscoe battled on as long as he could, but was compelled to surrender management of the bank and of his own affairs. As a banker, he proved himself extremely able, but he became the victim of circumstances beyond his control. The opening up of trade with America, following the end of the war brought great hopes of prosperity but in the short term created an instant demand for capital which, together with uncertainty and mistrust on the part of many clients, led to panic with the consequent withdrawal of huge sums of money.[116]

It was only by the allowance of a certificate of conformity that Roscoe's person could be protected from his creditors, and because this was delayed for several months, he was forced to take refuge in his lonely farm on Chat Moss between February and April 1820 and was obliged to stay indoors. Roscoe needed time to recover from the ordeal of bankruptcy and personal failure. What disappointed him most of all was not the loss of Allerton Hall and his many treasures, but his inability to fulfil his role as patron of the arts and of promising artists after the manner of his hero, Lorenzo de'Medici. He appears to have been separated from his wife and family for three or four months whether by choice or necessity. This was an anxious time for Jane and the family. In moments of depression he was sorely tempted to pass the rest of his days in the solitude of Chat Moss. After some hesitation he decided to return to Liverpool and pick up the threads of his former life. He wrote 'The struggle is now over ... in the circle of my own family, the society of my friends and the contracted limits of my literary pursuits, I shall look forward to the enjoyment of as much happiness as it is usual for human life to attain.[117] On his return home, without his knowledge, his friends collected the substantial sum of £2,500 for the benefit of himself and the family. Roscoe did consider going back to business, but owing to his state of health and his literary undertakings, he changed his mind, hoping to supplement his income out of writing.[118] During his self-imposed exile at Chat Moss, he devoted much of his time to the preparation for the press of his 'Illustrations Historical and Critical of the Life of Lorenzo de'Medici', intended as a reply to the criticisms of a French scholar, M. de Sismondi and others. The book was published in London and Edinburgh in 1822.

---

116   Memoir of Roscoe in his Life of Lorenzo, pages 41 et seq.

117   Life of W.R. Vol.2, pp.251-5.

118   Life of W.R. Vol.2, pp.251-5.

Roscoe's reputation as a writer was recognised by his election in 1819 as an honorary member of the Royal Society of Literature.[119] He was awarded the additional honour of Associate of the First Class, a body which included some of the most distinguished writers of his time. King George III generously arranged for a payment of 300 guineas to be made annually to the associates. Roscoe was classified as a writer of 'Literary History'. In 1827 he received further recognition, when he was awarded the Gold Medal for his merits as a historian. He was approached by an Edinburgh publisher, who invited him to write a history of the French Revolution.[120] This he would very much have liked to have undertaken, but felt it was to be too formidable a task for a man of his age. Sir Walter Scott was approached in his place, but declined the invitation, offering instead to write a biography of Napoleon Buonaparte, which was in fact published in 1827.

Soon after his return from Chat Moss, Roscoe with some friends published a new edition of the hymnal in use at the Renshaw Street Unitarian Chapel, of which he was a life-long member and worshipper.[121] Roscoe contributed nine new hymns written by himself. The religious motivation of Wilberforce was very different from that of Roscoe. Wilberforce, after his evangelical conversion declared his intention 'to stamp out slavery and raise the nation's morals'. Roscoe as a Dissenter and Unitarian was less dogmatic. His was a compassionate approach, based on an appreciation of God's love and providence. Roscoe, like Robert Burns, was not able to believe in a God who calls some and not others.[122] Roscoe's God is a God of majestic order - a transcendent God, glimpses of whom may be seen in the world of nature. He was a deeply religious man and God was never far from his thoughts. As a champion of liberty he upheld the sanctity of individual conscience. His religious outlook may well have been influenced by Neo-Platonism, which had become fashionable in Florence in the time of Lorenzo de Medici as well also as in 18th century England. The main purpose of the Neo-Platonists was to provide a sound and satisfactory intellectual basis for a rational life. Reason played a more prominent part than emotion in

---

119   Life of W.R. Vol.2, p.326.

120   Life of W.R. Vol.2, ch.15.

121   The congregation of the Renshaw Street Chapel moved to a new church in Ullett Road, and celebrated its tercentenary in 1991.

122   See Robert Burns' poem - 'Holy Willie's Prayer'.

every department of Roscoe's life. He knew how to cope with over-enthusiastic Christians like the Liverpool lady, who in 1820 sent him a copy of the Bible, 'expressing her respect for his character and her concern for his spiritual welfare'. He thanked her graciously for the gift, assuring her 'that he was not unacquainted with its contents'. He had, 'on more occasions than once, borne his humble testimony to their excellence, and had endeavoured, as far as lay in his power, to prevent their remaining a dead letter, by calling the precepts of the New Testament into practical use'. He asked her to do him the favour of perusing the concluding pages of a tract he had published in 1819 on the subject of Penal Jurisprudence and the Reformation of Criminals. He continued "The same sentiments, I have myself imbibed, have descended to my children and will, I trust, produce richer fruits".[123]

He enclosed with his letter a book of poems, written by his younger daughter Jane, expressing those religious sentiments and feelings of which he hoped his correspondent would approve.[124]

Soon after his return from Chat Moss and the sale of Allerton Hall, Roscoe, his wife and two daughters took up residence in Liverpool, first of all at Rake Lane (now Durning Road) and later at 5 St. James' Walk, where the Anglican Cathedral stands today.[125] In 1822 they settled into their new and final home in Lodge Lane. Roscoe spent much of his time writing. He was principally occupied with a new edition of the 'Works of Alexander Pope' which included a 'New Life of Pope' and an estimate of his poetical character and writings. This monumental work of ten volumes was published in 1824 in London.

In September of the same year, two years after settling into their new home, Jane Roscoe died. She had been in failing health for some time. The anxieties brought on by the long drawn-out financial troubles, the strain of moving from one house to another, the loss of their possessions and the care and upbringing of her large family must have taken a heavy toll on her health. Jane and William enjoyed forty years of happy and supportive married life.

---

123   Life of W.R. Vol.2, Ch.21, pp.442 and 443.

124   Frederick Warburton Dunston, Roscoeana, (Privately Printed). Jane published a book of poems in 1820, probably the book above mentioned. She also with her sister Mary Ann and others published a book entitled 'Poems for Youth' by a family circle 2 volumes (1820-1)'.

125   G.W. Mathews, Wm. Roscoe, p.38.

Roscoe's daughter, Jane,
author of a book of poems published in 1820

It was Fuseli who first introduced Roscoe to Mary Wollstonecraft, who shared his ideals of freedom and equality for dissenters.[126] Mary Wollstonecraft published in 1792 her 'Vindication of the Rights of Women' - a courageous attack on the conventions of the day. There is no evidence to suggest that Roscoe shared her views on women's liberation. Roscoe had a bee in his bonnet about bosoms and breast-feeding, which put into his head the idea of translating an Italian poem by Luigi Tansillo, entitled the Nurse, La Balia, into English verse. This gave rise to a good deal of ribaldry on the part of his critics, especially De Quincey, who dismissed the Nurse as 'a series of dullish lines for the purpose of persuading young women to suckle their own children.'[127] The Rev. Dr. Parr wrote 'I read Tansillo and was delighted'.[128] Chandler reminds us that in the dedicatory sonnet to his wife which was prefaced to 'The Nurse' in 1798, there is an un-English touch in the reference to the six sons successive and two daughters fair, who had drunk from his wife's breast.[129]

Henry, the youngest of the family and the faithful biographer of his father, arrived in 1799 too late to be mentioned in the sonnet. Roscoe's early romanticism gave way to an obsession with motherhood.

A stream of visitors and admirers from near and far called upon Roscoe in his home in his latter years. J.J. Audubon, having completed his portfolio of paintings and drawings of Birds of America made his journey to England from Louisiana, in order to exhibit and publish them. Soon after disembarking at Liverpool, he was invited to dine at the house of Richard Rathbone, where he met Roscoe and other friends and showed them his drawings. The following day he visited Roscoe in Lodge Lane. The entry in his Journal for July 27, 1826 gives us a vivid picture of his home-life in old age:

"I soon reach Mr. Roscoe's place, about one and a half miles distant (from Duke Street), a little drawing-room where all was Nature. This gentleman was drawing a very handsome plant very handsomely. The cabinet was ornamented with many other shrubs

126 Mary Wollstonecraft married William Godwin in 1797 and died at the birth of her daughter, Mary, the future Mrs. Shelley.

127 De Quincey, Reminiscences, Chapter 1.

128 Allibone, S.A. A Critical Dictionary of English Literature 1902, Vol.2, p.186-7.

129 G. Chandler, Roscoe of Liverpool - p.93.

receiving from his hands the care that Nature had insured them in their native climes, for I believe they were principally exotics from many distant and different parts of the world. The youngest daughter, the next, and the next, were alternately introduced to me. As it was too early to dine; it was proposed that we go to the Botanic Garden and the proposition was accepted immediately...

Now Mr. Roscoe is driving me in what he calls his little car, but the horse is so much less than what I conceived needed to pull it along with his master in that I was quite surprised to see the pony trot with both of us with apparent ease. Mr. Roscoe is ... one of those come-at-able persons that are just what is necessary for me to have to talk to. He is plain, kind, and prompt at bringing ease in his company.

Again in his charming laboratoire I look through windows that encompassed one full third of the oval, into a neat little garden. A glass of good wine is offered. It is drank, and my large portfolio is again on view ... Mr. Roscoe is anxious I should do well."[130]

All his life Roscoe had been interested in botany. He specialised in one particular branch, Monandrian plants of the order of Scitamineae and in 1828 published the result of his labours in a large folio volume, containing many beautiful plates by himself. His daughter-in-law, Margaret, Mrs. Edward Roscoe, assisted him in completing and preparing this work for the printer. This was the last of his publications.

Mrs. Hemans, whose writings were popular in America, and who is known in England as the author of 'Casabianca' (The Boy stood on the burning deck etc.) visited Roscoe in his last years. She described him as a delightful old man, with a fine Roman style of head, sitting in the study of his small house, surrounded by busts, books and flowers.[131]

As a result of his early concern regarding the evils of the Slave Trade and the growing commercial links between Liverpool and the New World, Roscoe developed a life-long interest in America, its people, its flora and fauna, its opportunities and problems. His tract entitled 'Observations on Penal Jurisprudence and the Reformation of Offenders' and two further

---

130 Journal of John James Audubon, 1826, pp.60-62 edited by Alice Ford, Norman, Oklahama, 1967.

131 F. Espinasse, Lancashire Worthies Vol.2, p.283, London, 1877.

works on the same subject attracted more interest in America than in Britain. In these writings he advocated a lessening of the severity of the penal code and pleaded that reformation, not vengeance, be the aim of all punishment.

Washington Irving, the first American man of letters to be internationally celebrated, gives us a portrait of Roscoe in 'The Sketch-Book'. He writes - "One of the first places to which a stranger is taken in Liverpool is the Athenaeum. As I was once visiting this haunt of the learned, my attention was drawn to a person just entering the room. He was advanced in life, tall and of a form that might once have been commanding, but it was a little bowed by time - perhaps by care. There was something in his whole appearance that indicated a being of a different order from the bustling race about him...

I inquired his name, and was informed that it was Roscoe. I drew back with an involuntary feeling of veneration. This then was an author of celebrity: this was one of those men whose voices have gone forth to the ends of the earth; with whose minds I have communed in the solitudes of America".[132]

One of many visitors who were made welcome by Roscoe in the last months of his life was a young journalist, James Mackay Wilson, from Berwick upon Tweed, who had established for himself something of a reputation as a local poet and as author of 'Wilson's Tales of the Borders' 6 volumes. Wilson in an article on 'Burns and Roscoe', in the Border Magazine,[133] gives a vivid account of his call at Roscoe's home, first informing his readers that:- 'There is one name that will ever go down to posterity in connexion with that of Burns. The name of William Roscoe, the patron of his family and friend of his Biographer; through whose exertions, the fame of Burns was made known to an English public, and provision made for his family.

... A few days after my arrival in Liverpool, in January 1831, I received an invitation from Mr. Roscoe. I found him seated by the fire, not in a very large, but the most tasteful library I ever saw. As I entered he smiling rose and extended his hand, and as he then stood, though somewhat bent in age, his stature could not be below six feet. A stroke of paralysis had

---

132   Washington Irving - The Sketch Book - Portrait of Roscoe, 1819, p.33.

133   The Border Magazine (Berwick upon Tweed) November 1831-1832 Vol.1, p.218 - Article
       on Burns and Roscoe.

rendered him very infirm, and slightly affected his features. His eyebrows were large and hanging, and faintly tinged with grey; but his grey eyes showed that even in age the sun of song was not set. He was dressed in sables after the manner of what may be termed a Briton in full dress, but wore upon his head a brown silk cap with a tassel descending to the ear. But his voice was tremulous and he moved with much difficulty. But his language, his actions and manners were gentle as a sweet tempered child. After listening to him with rapture upon several literary subjects, "See", said he, "You can walk better than I can. Take down those quarto volumes in blue morocco and examine them. They are a present of which I am very proud: and for typographical excellence, and elegant binding they are perhaps unequalled. And it is a most strange work; for it is merely a dissertation on the 'Correctness of the Text of De'Medici", by the Grand Duke of Tuscany - you know he is the same there as our king is here". Taking down the volumes, I found them edited by the Grand Duke of Tuscany in the original Italian and by him presented in token of esteem to the talented Roscoe.

"And what do you think of this?" added he, turning my attention to a huge elephant folio volume, "I commenced to write this after I was 73 years of age. I have always been fond of Botany, and the whole species of the plant on which it treats, grow in the garden before the window. It was a rather Herculean labour for an old man. And the drawings were by my daughter in law".

And after showing every thing which he thought could amuse me, he continued, "But I have reserved the best for the last, - open that portfolio with the green back, - and you will find a treasure, richer and dearer to me than all you have seen".

I opened it as desired, - and met with the unexpected delight of finding it contained several quires of the immortal Burns' original manuscript, which were presented to Roscoe by the poet's brother and widow in token of gratitude. Amongst them was the first he ever wrote, "The Twa Dogs", "Tam o'Shanter", and many others. The hand-writing, until the time of his being admitted to the Excise, was stiff, cramped and crooked. But after that period it assumes the appearance of a bold, dashing hand. On the margin were many remarks in the hand-writing of Gilbert Burns, by way of criticism: and particularly at Tam o'Shanter, I remarked these or similar words 'This is your best poem, your fame will greatly rest on it, G.B.'" The talented young journalist from the Scottish Borders remembered every moment spent with Roscoe.[134]

Another younger man to visit Roscoe in his last days was Johannan David Passavant (1787 to 1861), a German art historian and museum curator from Frankfurt, described 'as the first serious art historian'.[135] Passavant knew of Roscoe's European reputation as one of the few English art historians of the early part of the nineteenth century. He also knew that Roscoe and he had a certain amount in common, both having spent some years in business in provincial cities before devoting themselves to the arts and other cultural activities. Passavant was anxious to pay his respects to Roscoe, but he also had heard a rumour that Roscoe possessed some original letters by Raphael. Passavant was at that time 'embarking on the crowning stage of his life's work on Raphael'. Henry Roscoe, who in his biography of his father, mentions the names of several distinguished foreign visitors, who called upon Roscoe in the last months of his life, does not include Passavant's name on the list. Whether or not Roscoe himself knew of his existence is doubtful,but he received him with his customary courtesy. Passavant greatly appreciated the warmth of the welcome accorded to him, but was disappointed to find no original letters of Raphael and was astonished to discover that Roscoe had never set foot on Italy or even ventured as far as Paris. Roscoe and his daughter had the happy knack of making all their visitors respected and welcomed as the most important people in the world. The routine seems always to have included the proud display of the huge elephant folio volume containing Roscoe's botanical writings complete with drawings by his daughter - perhaps a gentle hint to suggest the visitor be on his way.

Passavant, much moved by his meeting with Roscoe and his daughter concluded his description of the event with these words:

'I congratulated myself on the happy chance which had made me witness of a scene of such innocent happiness as seemed to partake more of heaven than of earth. On taking leave, the excellent old man in the true hearty English style, shook me warmly by the hand, and, reminding me that he was not long for this world, gave me his parting blessing. His words were prophetic; before I reached London, he had peacefully passed to that world for which his spirit

---

134 Sadly James MacKay Wilson himself died at the age of 31 four years after his visit to Liverpool.

135 J.D. Passavant, Tour of a German Artist in England, reprint, ed. C.J. Bailey, 2 Vols. (Wakefield, 1978), ii, pp.12-17 and Edward Morris, Riches into Art, Liverpool Collectors 1770-1880 Liverpool University Press - Historical Essays, pp.7,8 and 9 et seq.

had here so ardently longed. His memory will always be sacred to me, and I am only thankful that the opportunity was granted me of knowing one who inspired affection and respect alike to all who, whether intimately or remotely, enjoyed that privilege.'

Shortly before his death, Roscoe formed another new if short-lived friendship. At an early age he wrote a small book to which he gave the title 'Christian Morality as contained in the Precepts of the New Testament - in the Language of Jesus Christ'. In his old age a book entitled 'the Precepts of Jesus' came to his notice, which bore a close resemblance to his own early work. The author of this book was a learned Brahmin, Rammohan Roy of Calcutta, who had become a convert to Christianity.[136] The object of the publication was to recommend the religion of Christ to the people of India. Roscoe was full of admiration for this native of India who had 'not only emancipated his mind from the dark and cruel superstitions in which he had been educated, but had cultivated his intellect to a degree which few of the natives of more favoured climes attain.'

In order to study the Scriptures Rammohan Roy had learnt Greek and Hebrew. The Brahmin was also deeply concerned for the welfare of his people and devoted himself to the extension of education and useful knowledge among them. He set up a printing press in Calcutta, at which his own work, 'the Precepts of Jesus' and other books designed to spread the Christian faith among 'Hindoos' were printed.[137]

Roscoe was determined to communicate with Rammohan Roy and asked a young friend, shortly to sail for India, to take out a letter and a selection of his own writings. Before the letter reached its destination, this remarkable Indian was on his way to Liverpool, where on arrival his striking appearance and character excited much curiosity and interest. After the usual gesture of eastern salutation, Rammohan Roy said: "Happy and proud am I to behold a man whose fame has extended not only over Europe, but over every part of the world".

"I bless God", replied Roscoe, "that I have been permitted to live to see this day."

Rammohan Roy and Roscoe discussed the reasons which brought Roy to Britain and in the course of their conversation he displayed an intimate knowledge of the political and commercial state of England. His stay in

---

136   Life of W.R. Vol.2, p.413.

137   Life of W.R. Vol.2, p.414 et seq.

*Raja Rammohan Roy - Roscoe's last and perhaps
most distinguished visitor - 'the Father of Modern India.'*

Liverpool had to be short, as Roy was anxious to be present in the House of Commons at the third reading of the Reform Bill and at the debate on India. Rammohan Roy took away with him a letter from Roscoe, commending him to Lord Brougham, who showed kindness to him in London.

Roscoe's meeting with Rammohan Roy was never forgotten by those who witnessed it. They would not have known that Rammohan Roy was to go down to history as 'the Father of Modern India'.[138] Both Roscoe and Rammohan Roy were pioneers of liberal reform in their respective countries. Whilst Roscoe was campaigning for the abolition of the slave trade, Rammohan Roy pioneered a movement for the abolition of sati (suttee). Rammohan Roy and Roscoe had much in common. Both were attracted by Christian ethics rather than by Christian dogma. Both held basically Unitarian views, which Rommahan Roy believed could be combined with an enlightened and reformed Hinduism.

George Chandler, in his volume published for the bi-centenary of Roscoe's birth, suggests that Roscoe's approach to painting and poetry pointed the way that Ruskin was to follow.[139] In certain respects Ruskin and Roscoe had much in common: in others they were poles apart. Venice was to Ruskin what Florence was to Roscoe. Ruskin by frequent visits knew every stone in Venice; Roscoe's knowledge of Florence was second-hand. Both idealised the cities they espoused. Both held a moralistic and historical view, believing that Britain had much to learn from the rise and fall of these model city states. Ruskin had the benefit of an academic education at Oxford as well as the best tuition available in drawing and painting, becoming the first Slade Professor of Art at Oxford in 1869, whilst Roscoe was a selftaught amateur. Of the two Ruskin was the more romantic, prolific and polished writer.

In his essay, Riches into Art, Edward Morris describes Roscoe as 'an oddity in Liverpool' and goes on to say that 'Liverpool was an odd place

---

138 Robin Boyd. Introduction to Indian Christian Theology, 1969 C.L.S. pages 19 and 21.
    The turning-point in Rammohan Roy's life came in 1811 when he was the unwilling witness of the suttee of his brother's wife. The incident made him vow to devote his life to the overthrow of this and similar abuses. Suttee is the custom, whereby every Hindu widow was obliged to throw herself on to her late husband's funeral pyre. Rammohan Roy sailed to England in 1830 on a visit which brought him great fame and popularity. He hoped to return to India for further service of his people but died in Bristol in 1833.

139 George Chandler, William Roscoe of Liverpool, 1953, p.98.

for him to be in.'[140] Ruskin, an oddity in his youth, became increasingly eccentric as the years passed. In 1856 Ruskin made the pronouncement that 'the clear and tasteless poison of the art of Raphael ... infects the hearts of millions of Christians.'[141] Claiming to have discovered Carpaccio, Ruskin described one of his less distinguished paintings in Venice, known as the Two Courtesans, as the best picture in the world.[142] Ruskin was inobservant not noticing the coat of arms of the highly respectable Venetian family to which the ladies belonged.[143] In the same way Roscoe was equally inobservant not recognising the wrong coat of arms and even the wrong church in a painting, which he deluded himself into thinking contained portraits of three generations of the Medici family.[144] Latterly Ruskin took a deeply pessimistic view of the future of Venice and Britain, whereas Roscoe clung steadfastly to his belief in progress, a humanist and humanitarian, maintaining a lively interest in and respect for individual human beings as well as human rights to a ripe old age.

In 1827 Roscoe's family and friends became increasingly anxious about his health. He had suffered two or three strokes causing a loss of memory and a difficulty in speech, but his mental faculties were unimpaired, enabling him to continue writing. Shortly before his death he confided in his friend and physician, Dr. Traill, saying - "He thanked God, the Almighty, for having permitted him to pass a life of much happiness, which, though somewhat checkered by vicissitude,had been on the whole one of great enjoyment; and he trusted that he should be enabled cheerfully to resign it whenever it pleased God to call him."[145] Henry, his son and biographer, tells us that 'in this tranquil and happy frame of mind he continued to the last'. Following a severe attack of 'flu, Roscoe died on June 27, 1831.

---

140   Edward Morris, Liverpool Historical Essays, Riches into Art, p.26.

141   The Cook and Wedderburn edition of Ruskin's 'Modern Painters', Vol.5, p.84.

142   John Ruskin, St. Mark's Rest see E.V. Lucas, A. Wanderer in Venice, p.38.

143   Allilia Dorigato, Carpaccio, Bellini, Antonella dalla Pinacoteca de Museo Correr, Milan 1993 pp.74 to 79. The upper part of this painting by Carpaccio, now in the J. Paul Getty Museum, Malibu, entitled Caccia in Laguna, depicts the husbands engaged in a duck-shooting expedition in the lagoon, while their Venetian wives patiently await their return.

144   William Roscoe, Illustrations Historical and Critical of the Life of Lorenzo, 1822 page 89 - see also Edward Morris, 'Riches into Art' pages 14 and 15 and print of the painting 'San Bernardino Preaching'.

145   Life of W.R., Vol.2, ch.21, pp.420 et seq. and Dr. Traill's Memoir.

The funeral took place at the Renshaw Street Chapel, and the interment in the burial ground close by in the heart of the city he loved and served so well.

Perhaps the most tangible and enduring legacy of Roscoe to Liverpool was the planning, along with Dr. Traill, and the opening of the Royal Institution, as an adult educational centre in 1817.[146] Roscoe, as President, delivered an address, setting forth his ideals of what the Institution might become as a centre of scholarship, learning and the arts. Out of the Royal Institution sprang a well-known school and, sixty-five years later, the foundation of the University College, which in turn became the University of Liverpool. After Roscoe's death, Dr Traill who, apart from the family, knew him more intimately than any others, in making an assessment of Roscoe's character and achievements, wrote 'I may be permitted to state my conviction, that had he been left to pursue his original plan of literary retirement, instead of again plunging into the cares and anxieties of business, he would have left behind a work on the History of the Fine Arts, far superior to anything on that subject which British literature possesses.'[147]

Dr. Traill did not know that the era of the amateur scholar and historian was shortly to give way to that of the professional expert. Roscoe has been designated a generalist rather than a specialist.[148] The generalist tends to be a more interesting character than the specialist, despite the fact that the latter has become indispensable. Alexander Pope, for whom Roscoe had a high regard, stressed the disadvantages of too superficial a knowledge, when he wrote:

> 'A little learning is a dangerous thing;
>
> Drink deep, or taste not the Pierian spring;
>
> There shallow draughts intoxicate the brain,
>
> And drinking largely sobers us again.[149]

This was, of course, Roscoe's problem. His brain became easily intoxicated by shallow draughts of knowledge - hence his wild and uncritical enthusiasm for Lorenzo the Magnificent, for which his friend Fuseli constantly chaffed him.

---

146   Sydney Jones. Address at the opening of the Roscoe Centenary Exhibition in 1931.

147   Dr. Thomas Stewart Traill, Memoir of William Roscoe, page 28. 1832 - reprinted from Edinburgh New Philosophical Journal No.26.

148   Edward Morris, Riches into Art, page 12.

149   Pope, Essay on Criticism II, line 215.

Another defect in Roscoe's character was largely caused by the fact that he was ill at ease when away from his native city and his home. This showed itself in a certain lack of self-confidence combined with a measure of irritability, which William Rathbone warned him to guard against. Roscoe had expensive tastes and was teased by Rathbone for his extravagance.[150] Money, as such, meant little to him. It was not so much the loss of money or even of possessions, but his inability to continue in his role as patron of the arts, which hit him hardest after his bankruptcy. Whilst Roscoe had no hesitation in cultivating friends in high places, sending them copies of his books or gifts of the best early Lancashire potatoes,[151] he was utterly free from snobbery, mixing easily in all classes of society. He was happiest in his own home, surrounded by his family and devoted to his wife, Jane, who was a pillar of strength to him throughout their married life.

A young admirer of Roscoe, Joseph Mayer, who became a successful manufacturing jeweller, art collector and connoisseur, almost certainly frequented the Royal Institution, which comprised a library, meeting rooms and art gallery. Although very different in character and background, Roscoe and Mayer had much in common as patrons of art and benefactors of Liverpool. Mayer was a knowledgeable Egyptologist and many of his treasures are to be seen in the Walker Art Gallery in Liverpool today. Roscoe appears to have shared his interest in Egyptology.[152] In 1823 Roscoe and Dr Noehdin of the British Museum were asked to select an Egyptian mummy at the Egyptian Hall in Piccadilly, owned by Mr William Bullock, a showman and dealer in antiquities. The mummy was to be presented to the Leeds Philosophical and Literary Society for display in the society's newly established museum. The choice proved a good one. It consisted of a fully preserved Egyptian mummy, originally filched from a cemetery at Thebes, which was conveyed first to Trieste and on to London. On arrival at Leeds after a thorough scientific and medical investigation, the mummy was discovered to be that Natsef-Amun, a Priest in the Temple of Karnak. There appears to have been no limit to Roscoe's curiosity and interests even in his old age. Those were the days when local museums became the rage and no museum was complete without a Mummy!

---

150   Roscoe Papers 3059. Letter from William Rathbone to Roscoe dated December 13 1796.

151   Roscoe Papers 1743 - Letter of thanks dated March 1805, sent on behalf of Prince William of Gloucester for the gift of Lancashire potatoes, 'which he will eat with special pleasure as a gift from Roscoe'.

152   The Leeds Intelligencer, February 2, 1824 and March 17, 1824 - also A.R. David and E. Tapp, The Mummy's Tale, Michael O'Mara Books Limited.

Joseph Mayer in Clarence Terrace on the Roscoe Chair,
c. 1840.
by William Daniels, Liverpool Museum (WAG 7355).
reproduced by courtesy of NMGM

After Roscoe's death Mayer believed that the mantle of Roscoe had fallen on his shoulders, as is evident from the portrait of himself enthroned on what came to be called the 'Roscoe Chair'.[153] Joseph Mayer, according to Margaret Gibson, 'could read a catalogue though he could not write a book.'[154] Yet his assessment of Roscoe's place in history and in the life of his native city is perhaps the best of all:"

> He who would treat of any movement in Liverpool, political, social or aesthetic at the end of the Eighteenth Century must needs allude to this extraordinary man... Born in any age, his talents, his conscientious industry and his patient intelligence, would have earned him place and name... Roscoe's honour lies not so much in deeds of his own excellent and admirable as they were - as in those which he caused others to do. A leading man amongst people who regarded business as the one aim of life and title to respect, he boldly proclaimed another and nobler ideal... He interested the public and thus ensured a succession of disciples to labour in the cause after his own decease."[155]

---

153 See the Painting of Joseph Mayer in Clarence Terrace c.1840 by William Daniels, the Liverpool Museum (WAG 7355). Margaret Gibson, F.S.A. in her Essay on Joseph Mayer 1803-1886 describes him as 'seated in the Roscoe chair, contemplating a Wedgewood urn, carelessly fingering a learned pamphlet, the light falling on classical marbles, and on the table Greek and Etruscan antiquities'.

154 Joseph Mayer of Liverpool, ed. Margaret Gibson and Susan M. Wright (Longman 1988)

155 G.W. Mathews - 'William Roscoe', p.46.

Chapter Two

Roscoe's Writings
Biography of Lorenzo de' Medici

Thomas De Quincey, diarist and author of many literary works, including the 'Confessions of an Opium Eater', as a precocious teenager was invited by William Clarke to attend meetings of the Liverpool coterie, of which Roscoe was the acknowledged leader.[1] He was even privileged to dine with the group and to join in discussions, despite the fact that he had run away from the Manchester Grammar School, later leaving Oxford without a degree. Sir Alfred Shennan, in his introduction to George Chandler's volume published for the Roscoe bicentenary, reminded us that De Quincey returned the hospitality accorded to him by the group by writing 'a grossly disparaging account of their company' in Tait's Edinburgh Magazine in 1837. Edward Sackville West described the account as 'waspish'.[2] Later De Quincey wrote a shade more generously of Roscoe, but the sting was not removed. He referred to Roscoe as one who possessed 'the feebleness of a mere belle-lettrist'.[3] Though a prolific writer, Roscoe showed little sign of feebleness. If a belle-lettrist is a writer whose chief merit is elegance and style rather than content, De Quincey misjudged him. A man of many talents, Roscoe felt impelled to share his varied interests and concerns with others, expressing himself lucidly and often with vigour in prose and verse. His writings like those of many of his contemporaries, tend to be verbose and pompous at times, but not unduly so. His comments on people and affairs are often shrewd and surprisingly terse.

---

1   William Roscoe of Liverpool, George Chandler, 1953 - the Introduction by Sir Alfred Shennan page xxii et seq.

2   Edward Sackville West, A Flame in Sunlight, London 1936, pp.38 and 39.

3   William Roscoe of Liverpool by George Chandler. Introduction by Shennan p.xxxv.

Life of Lorenzo de' Medici

It was Roscoe's 'Life of Lorenzo de' Medici, called the Magnificent', published in 1796, which won him fame as a writer. Some admirers of Roscoe have tended to think of him as an eminent Liverpool merchant banker and patron of the arts, who in his leisure hours wrote a life of Lorenzo the Magnificent.[4] Sir John Hale, the historian, has rightly reminded us that it was before Roscoe became widely known and respected in Liverpool that he became recognised as one of the greatest scholars of his time, whose name was as internationally famous as Gibbon.[5] Roscoe's fame and reputation as a historian and scholar, like his wealth, were meteoric. What is remarkable is that an industrious self-taught scholar, son of a Liverpool innkeeper, should have ever risen to such great heights at all. In his rise and in his fall he made his mark and challenged others to look at the Medici and the Republic of Florence and the Italian Renaissance more objectively.

Roscoe became convinced of the need for 'a complete history of the period',[6] but soon realised that this was a task beyond his powers, much as he would have liked to have undertaken it himself. 'A mind of greater compass and the possession of uninterrupted leisure were an essential requisite for anyone expecting to comprehend, to select and arrange the immeasurable variety of circumstances, which a full narrative of those times would involve'. Roscoe confessed himself 'rather dazzled than informed' by the prospect.

Having put aside any thought of writing a comprehensive history of the period, Roscoe focused his attention on the Medici family in Florence and in particular upon Lorenzo de' Medici, its most distinguished member. Florence under the Medici had become a new Athens, an ideal society presided over by a dynasty of cultured bankers. Might not the same thing happen in England, perhaps even in Liverpool? Sixty years later, in 1854, Queen Victoria, when she first set eyes on the newly built St. George's Hall at the opening ceremony, declared it to be 'worthy of ancient Athens'.[7]

---

4   C.P. Darcy, discussing Roscoe's 'Life of Lorenzo' in his book 'The Encouragement of the Fine Arts in Lancashire', 1760 to 1860, informs us that the work was 'one banker's tribute to another' - a statement which is inaccurate, because Roscoe unwillingly took up banking after its publication.

5   J.R. Hale, England and the Italian Renaissance, page 89.

6   William Roscoe, Life of Lorenzo de' Medici, Preface pages 7 et seq.

Terracotta bust of Lorenzo de' Medici, by Verrocchio
(National Gallery of Art, Washington)

Roscoe made it clear in his preface to the 'Life of Lorenzo' that his intention was not to confine himself 'merely to the relation of the life of an individual however illustrious, but to give some account of the rise of the Medici family and the principal events in and affecting Florence during Lorenzo's lifetime.[8] Roscoe began to write soon after the publication of Edward Gibbon's monumental work, his 'History of the Decline and Fall of the Roman Empire', in 1788, a work which necessitated twenty years of laborious research and writing. The last chapter of 'The Decline and Fall' was in the forefront of his mind when in the preface to the Life of Lorenzo Roscoe wrote: 'under the auspices of the House of Medici, and particularly through the ardour and example of Lorenzo, the empire of science and true taste was again restored'.[9]

Roscoe was firmly of the opinion that 'no man was ever more admired and venerated by his contemporaries, or has been more defrauded of his just fame by posterity, than Lorenzo de' Medici'.[10] Soon after Lorenzo's death a short biography was written in Latin by his friend and contemporary Niccolo Valori. This work was translated into Italian in 1560.[11] Roscoe relied on Valori's 'accurate account of the principal events of Lorenzo's life', but complained that the book 'gives us too distant and indistinct a view of Lorenzo himself, and lacks the interest which might have been derived from a closer and more intimate examination of the temper, character and writing of Lorenzo'.[12] Roscoe had access to and more likely was able to obtain for himself copies of contemporary histories. Apart from Valori these included the Florentine histories of Machiavelli, and Ammirato and the critical works of Crescimbeni, Muratori, Bandini and Tiraboschi and some other writings of lesser importance, to all of which constant reference is made throughout the book.[13] Without the help of these histories and Valori's biography, Roscoe would have been unable to complete the first volume of his work before the return from Florence in the spring of 1790 of William Clarke, bringing

---

7   Peter Aughton - Liverpool - A People's History, 1990, page 163.

8   Wm. Roscoe, Life of Lorenzo, Preface page 10 (Bohn edition).

9   Wm. Roscoe, Life of Lorenzo, Preface pp.8 and 9. (Bohn edition).

10   Wm. Roscoe, Life of Lorenzo, Preface pp.8 and 9 (Bohn edition).

11   William Roscoe, Life of Lorenzo, Preface pages 10 and 11.

12   William Roscoe, Life of Lorenzo, Preface pages 10 and 11.

13   Life of W.R. Vol.1 page 145 and Life of Lorenzo by Wm. Roscoe, Preface, p.14.

with him the fruits of his researches, including manuscripts, information, archives and copies of documents. Clarke had already promised to hand over on arrival at Liverpool two works by Monsignor Fabroni, an Italian scholar, written in Latin - his 'Life of Lorenzo de'Medici', published in 1784 and his 'Life of Cosimo de'Medici', Lorenzo's grandfather, published also in Pisa in 1789. After reading Fabroni's 'Life of Lorenzo', Roscoe found himself in a quandary. Was it really worth while for him to proceed with his cherished project, or should he abandon it altogether and content himself with making an English translation of Fabroni's excellent work?'[14] Roscoe decided to proceed with his biography undeterred. He came to the conclusion that 'the leading object of Fabroni is to illustrate the political rather than the literary life of Lorenzo'.[15] He believed his own fellow countrymen would be more interested 'in the progress of letters and arts under Lorenzo than in the more historical events of the fifteenth century so far as they regarded Italy.[16] Fabroni's 'Life of Lorenzo' was based on a thorough research of relevant documents from archives in Florence. Roscoe benefitted greatly by being able, with the help of William Clarke, to identify and use the same sources in preparing his own work.[17]

When the first volume of Roscoe's 'Life of Lorenzo' was nearly printed and materials were being arranged for completion of the second, he obtained a copy of an unfinished work entitled 'Memoires Genealogiques de la Maison de Medici', originally written in French by a Dutchman, Nicholas Tenhove of the Hague. This remarkable work was translated into English by Sir Richard Clayton Bt. and published in two volumes in 1797 in Bath. It included notes and observations by the translator. Clayton dedicated his work to the Marquis of Lansdowne, who probably supplied him with one of the original French copies of these memoirs. Clayton tells us that the Memoirs of the House of Medici 'were composed by Tenhove at his Ease from time to time and were printed Piece-meal as they were composed' and that 'in the form he left them, have rather the aspect of interesting Materials for a great Work than that of a regular Edifice.[18] As he did not live to complete the Design, he committed to the flames all the copies of those memoirs, excepting those which he had

---

14 William Roscoe, Life of Lorenzo, Preface page 15.
15 Wm. Roscoe, Life of Lorenzo, Preface pp.15 and 16.
16 Wm. Roscoe, Life of Lorenzo, Preface pp.15 and 16.
17 Wm. Roscoe, Life of Lorenzo, Preface pp.15 and 16.
18 Nicholas Tenhove, Memoirs of the House of Medici translated by Sir Richard Clayton, Bt. 1797, Preface pp.2 and 3.

distributed to his particular Friends'. Clayton described Tenhove 'as a shy and timid man, but that in the small circle of his intimate friends and acquaintances his exquisite Wit and Humour had their free course, made Laughter hold both his Sides, and were an inexhaustible Source of Entertainment to his Friends'. He also tells us that 'an easy fortune and a previous stock of classical and historical knowledge rendered him capable of deriving signal advantages from his travels in Italy and Sicily, where he observed the sublime and elegant productions of nature and art with the taste and enthusiasm of an enlightened connoisseur.'

Roscoe had the opportunity to read and study Tenhove's - 'Memoirs of the House of Medici' before the publication of his own 'Life of Lorenzo' in 1796.[19] He felt in no way threatened by the publication of Tenhove's work. He described the latter as 'rather the amusement of the leisure hours of a polite scholar than the research of a profound historian.' He reckoned it to be 'the most engaging work that has ever appeared on a subject of literary history, written by a native of one country, in the language of another on the affairs of a third.'[20]

Roscoe claimed not to have derived any important help from his study of Tenhove's Memoirs of 'the House of Medici', pointing out that whilst it was the intention of Tenhove to tell the story of the Medici family from the remotest antiquity to the present day, he intended to confine himself to Lorenzo and the period in which he lived. Roscoe's Life of Lorenzo, in its format, bears a remarkable similarity to Clayton's translation of Tenhove's Memoirs. Roscoe in his preface tells us that Tenhove's valuable Life of Lorenzo extended to as many as twenty-three chapters, but that he had confined himself to no more than thirteen, adding a summary of the contents of each chapter together with notes and observations of his own. There are notable differences and similarities between these works. Roscoe took himself much more seriously than Tenhove, whose sparkling sense of humour enlivens many a page.

---

19 Clayton did not publish his translation of Tenhove until after the publication of Roscoe's biography of Lorenzo. Roscoe must have been given a proof copy of Tenhove's work long before it was actually published in its final form in 1797. Clayton's Translation of Tenhove's Memoirs contains references to **Roscoe's** work. It seems unlikely that Roscoe had one of the original copies of Tenhove in French.

20 Wm. Roscoe, Life of Lorenzo, Preface page 17 (Bohn Edition).

It is worth asking ourselves at this point how far Roscoe was disadvantaged in writing his Life of Lorenzo by his unwillingness or inability to travel in Italy. Sir John Hale expresses surprise that 'Roscoe did not find an undue restlessness at devoting years of thought to a country he would never see.'[21] He also tells us that Roscoe was not alone in his belief that 'a writer need not visit the country he was concerned with.' It is easy to forget that the opportunity for foreign travel, in any degree of safety or comfort in the eighteenth century, was only available to the wealthy and adventurous. Even if Roscoe had been wealthy enough as a young man to make the journey to Florence, it is more than doubtful whether he would have been any more successful than William Clarke in collecting materials and information. Roscoe lacked experience in reading manuscripts and ancient documents and his limited knowledge of languages other than Italian and English, made his task all the more difficult. Certainly a visit to Italy might have saved him the embarrassment of making serious mistakes and have given him a truer picture of life in Renaissance Florence, but this might not have made a substantial difference to the work itself. Tenhove's 'Memoirs of the House of Medici' benefit not only from his thorough grounding in the classics but also from his travels, which add colour and authenticity to his writing. What is remarkable is that Roscoe's Life of Lorenzo was destined to become immensely popular for many years, whereas Tenhove's Memoirs have remained little known and appreciated only by a few. Historians and writers who lived in days before easy travel and dared to write well about countries they had never visited, deserve to be respected and not anathematized.[22]

It is not altogether surprising that, though Roscoe had finished the first volume of his 'Life of Lorenzo' by the time William Clarke returned from Italy in the spring of 1790, the work was not completed and published until 1796. Throughout the time of writing Roscoe was heavily engaged in his legal practice, in public affairs and with family responsibilities. The 'Life of Lorenzo', the work of an enthusiastic, painstaking but untutored amateur, did fulfil the hopes and expectations

---

21 England and The Italian Renaissance, J.R. Hale, chapter 4, pp.96 and 97.

22 England and The Italian Renaissance, J.R. Hale, page 97.

'Taine anathematised Grote for writing a history of Greece without setting foot there'.

Cosimo de' Medici,
by Verrocchio

(courtesy of Staatliche Museum, Berlin)

of many in Britain, who wanted to know more about the glory of Florence under the Medici. It consists of a straight-forward, if somewhat rambling account of the rise of the Medici and their achievements. It covers a wide field and is the result of careful research as is made evident by reference to his sources of information at the foot of almost every page, and, as if that was not enough at the end of the book there are a further eighty closely packed pages made up of three hundred and fifty two notes supplementing the text. Roscoe enjoyed the freedom to write about the things which appealed to him most.

The first chapter gives an indication of the width of Roscoe's interests and the scope of the book. Within thirty pages he managed to cover the origins of Florence, the rise of the Medici family, Giovanni de'Medici and his son Cosimo, who laid the foundation of the family's greatness, the revival of Platonic philosophy, the invention and progress of the art of printing, the establishment of the Laurentian Library, the Library of S. Marco and the Vatican Library, the general council held in Florence in 1439 under Pope Eugenius IV preparatory to a proposed union of the Orthodox and Roman churches, the Fall of Constantinople, the marriage of Lorenzo's parents, Lorenzo's birth and finally the death and character of Cosimo, his grand-father.

Cosimo, of all the Medici, was the one with whom one might have expected Roscoe to have had most in common. Francesco Guicciardini, designated by Sir John Hale as the greatest historian between Tacitus in the first century and Voltaire and Gibbon in the eighteenth,[23] has left us a characteristically down-to-earth comparison between the greatness of Cosimo and the greatness of Lorenzo, with which Roscoe must have been familiar. Guicciardini believed that:-

'Cosimo had greater wisdom and judgement than Lorenzo. Cosimo, although he had many cares of state, did not neglect commerce and private affairs; rather he managed them with so much diligence and skill that his wealth was always greater than the state, which was enormous, and he was never forced to manipulate the income of the state or to usurp private fortunes. The generosity of both was immense, but in different fields. Cosimo was lavish in building palaces and churches in and outside Florence, and things which should last and perpetuate

---

23 F. Guicciardini, The History of Florence, English Translation by Cecil Grayson, 1964, introduction by J.R. Hale page VII.

in itself but compared with the innumerable works of Cosimo, it seems next to nothing. However he was a great patron and with his gifts and liberality he achieved great friendships with princes and with men who served them. On these grounds I conclude that when everything is weighed, Cosimo was a more able man; nevertheless both were so eminent in virtue and fortune that perhaps since the fall of Rome, Italy has had no private citizen to compare with them.'[24]

Roscoe tells us that it was Cosimo who 'in affording protection to the arts of architecture, painting and sculpture, which then began to revive in Italy, set the example to those who by their riches could alone afford effectual aid.'[25] He was greatly impressed by the fact that the patronage Cosimo offered was extended in a different spirit from that normally shown by the rich to the poor; rather it was a patronage based on genuine friendship and equal partnership in a task - the task of embellishing their native city. Roscoe was equally impressed by the fact that Cosimo had no hesitation in turning down Brunelleschi's design of a palace 'which might have suited the proudest sovereign in Europe' in favour of a much less elaborate plan of Michellozzi, 'which united extent with simplicity and elegance with convenience'.[26]

In many ways Cosimo seems to have been a more attractive character than his grandson, more prepossessing in appearance, more dignified, more prudent, friendly and democratic. Perhaps it was the flamboyant side of Lorenzo's character, his prowess as an athlete, his skill in a tournament, his poetic genius, his love of spectacle, his extravagance and licentiousness which secretly intrigued Roscoe most.

Roscoe tells us that Cosimo, on his return to Florence from his ten years' banishment to Padua and Venice, enjoyed a life of uninterrupted prosperity and tranquillity.[27] It was a period during which 'the pursuits of the opulent were directed rather towards the recovery of the works of the ancients (Greek and Roman authors) than towards the encouragement of contemporary merit.[28] Precious manuscripts were 'daily perishing in

---

24   F. Guicciardini, The History of Florence, English Translation by Cecil Grayson, 1964, introduction by J.R. Hale pages IX and X.
25   Life of Lorenzo, Wm. Roscoe, chapter 1, page 77.
26   Life of Lorenzo, Wm. Roscoe (Bohn), page 77.
27   Wm. Roscoe, Life of Lorenzo, page 58.
28   Wm. Roscoe, Life of Lorenzo, page 60.

obscure corners, a prey to oblivion and neglect'. Cosimo made full use of his commercial contacts in Europe and Asia Minor in his efforts to collect and preserve manuscripts of classical writers, encouraging and often financing scholars, missionaries, preachers and other travellers on their journeys to remote countries in search of these treasures. Roscoe, for lack of space, resisted the temptation to tell the full story of those courageous scholar-adventurers who regarded 'the discovery of an ancient manuscript as almost the equivalent of the conquest of a kingdom.'[29]

Roscoe tells us at the beginning of chapter 4 that 'Whilst Lorenzo was dividing his time between the cares of government and the promotion of literature, an event took place that attracted the attention of all Italy towards Milan.'[30] The event was the assassination in 1476 of Duke Galeazza Maria Sforza in a solemn procession, and in his ducal robes, as he was entering the Church of S. Stefano. The excitement of all this had scarcely died away when a similar event took place on Easter Day in 1478 at Florence of 'a much more atrocious nature'. The event proved to be a significant turning-point in Lorenzo's life as well as in his character. He knew that in every generation plots had been made to ruin his family, but had not allowed this knowledge to interfere with the enjoyment of his youth. After the Pazzi conspiracy, which resulted in the murder of Giuliano, Lorenzo's brother, and the wounding of Lorenzo himself, he was compelled to concentrate above all else on the security and survival of the Medici family at the cost of his own popularity.

Roscoe after drawing his readers' attention to Voltaire's observation to the effect that the conspiracy 'is an incontrovertible proof of the practical atheism of the times in which it took place,'[31] has given us a lively and detailed account of the whole affair, describing it as 'a transaction in which a pope, a cardinal, an archbishop and several other ecclesiastics, associated themselves with a band of ruffians to destroy two men who were an honour to their age and country; and purposed to perpetrate their crime at a season of hospitality, in the sanctuary of a Christian church, and at the moment of the elevation of the host, when the audience bowed down before it, and the assassins were presumed to be in the immediate presence of God.'[32]

---

29 Wm. Roscoe, Life of Lorenzo, page 60.

30 Wm. Roscoe, Life of Lorenzo, chapter 4, p.137.

31 Voltaire, Essai sur les Moeurs, ii, p.283, Ed. Geneva 1760.

32 Wm. Roscoe, Life of Lorenzo, chapter 4, page 139.

Chapter 5 of the Life of Lorenzo is outstanding. It contains a lucid account of the development of Italian literature from the XlVth century, the fruit of nearly twenty years of study. Roscoe's writing clearly indicates his firm grasp of the basic principles underlying the art of poetry and his familiarity with the works of Dante, Petrarch, Boccaccio and other Italian poets. He then proceeds to discuss in detail Lorenzo's writings and in particular his poetry. He quotes a letter from Lorenzo to Ficino, in which Lorenzo wrote, 'When my mind is disturbed with the tumults of public business and my ears are stunned with the clamours of turbulent citizens, how would it be possible for me to support such contention, unless I found a relaxation in science?[33]

Roscoe explained that in Lorenzo's younger days 'the science' for which he had a preference was 'poetry'. Roscoe could readily identify himself with Lorenzo, both in his desire for peace and leisure for literary pursuits and in his early preference for poetry.

Lorenzo was aware that the indulgence of his poetic taste might be regarded as a sign of levity for one in his position.[34] Giovanni della Mirandola quoted Lorenzo as having said in self-defence, 'Persecuted as I have been from my youth, some indulgence may perhaps be allowed me for having sought consolation in such pursuits.'[35] Roscoe tells us that Lorenzo began to exercise his talent for poetry at a very young age, having been asked by Federigo d'Aragona, on his way from Naples to Burgundy, when he visited Pisa, to recommend such pieces of Italian poetry as were deserving of his attention. At the age of seventeen Lorenzo prepared a volume containing his selection adding some 'songs' and sonnets of his own composition, and sent it to the prince as a testimony of his affection and regard.[36] For his part Roscoe at an early age had made a selection from the works of the popular poets of his day of whom Shenstone held pride of place in the collection, and in which Goldsmith and Collins also appeared among the favourites.[37] Several original poems by Roscoe himself were, of course, inserted in the

---

33   William Roscoe - Life of Lorenzo de Medici, chapter 5, p.169.

34   William Roscoe, Life of Lorenzo de'Medici (Bohn), p.170.

35   In Proem, ad tract, de ente et uno in op. Pici. ed. Ven 1498 see page 170 as above, footnote.

36   William Roscoe, Life of Lorenzo, page 177 and page 511, note 151.

37   Wm. Roscoe - Life, of Lorenzo, Ch. V, page 178.

A page from Roscoe's Select Poems from Several Authors, vol. 2 p. 203. A favourite poem entitled 'La Solitude', by Saint-Amant, 1594 - 1661, a French metaphysical poet, in his own hand-writing illustrated with a delightful drawing of his own at the age of seventeen.

(Record Office, Central Library, Liverpool).

manuscript volumes. Roscoe thinking of his own experience as a boy, remarked that 'the simple description of natural objects is perhaps to the young mind the most delightful species of poetry and was probably the first employment of the poet (Lorenzo).'[38]

He singled out three examples of Lorenzo's accurate descriptions of the face of nature, the first two from his poem 'Ambra'.[39] The first is a vivid picture of olive trees, the leaves shimmering in the soft west wind and the second is of migrating cranes in flight:-[40]

> L' uliva, in qualche dolce piaggia aprica,
> Secondo il vento par, or verde, or bianca.

> On some sweet sunny slope the olive grows,
> Its hues still changing as the zephyr blows.

*   *   *   *   *

> Stridendo in ciel, i gru veggonsi a lunge
> L'aere stampar di varie e belle forme;
> E l' ultima col collo steso aggiunge
> Ov'è quella dinanzi alle vane orme.

> Marking the tracts of air, the clamorous cranes
> Wheel their due flight, in varied lines descried;
> And each with outstretched neck his rank maintains,
> In marshalled order through th'ethereal void.

---

38 Wm. Roscoe - Life of Lorenzo, Ch. V, page 178.

39 Lorenzo's Poem - 'Ambra' is printed on page 373 in the Bohn edition of Roscoe's 'Life of Lorenzo'.

40 The Italian originals are followed by Roscoe's translations into English.

The third example is a delightful pastoral scene from Lorenzo's poem -
Selve d'Amore,[41] which expresses Lorenzo's love of his native Tuscan
countryside and his keen awareness of its beauties:

> Al dolce tempo il bon pastore informa
>
> Lasciar le mandre, ove nel verno giacque:
>
> E'l lieto gregge, che ballando in torma,
>
> Torna all'alte montagne, alle fresche acque.
>
> L'agnel, trottando pur la materna orma
>
> Segue; ed alcun, che pur or ore nacque,
>
> L'amorevol pastore in braccio porta:
>
> Il fido cane a tutti fa la scorta.

> Sweet spring returns; the shepherd from the fold
>
> Brings forth his flock, nor dreads the wintry cold;
>
> Delighted once again their steps to lead
>
> To the green hill, clear spring, and flowery mead.
>
> True to their mother's track, the sportive young
>
> Trip light, the careful hind slow moves along,
>
> Pleased in his arms the new-dropt lamb to bear;
>
> His dog, a faithful guard, brings up the rear.

Roscoe found himself comparing Lorenzo's work with that of Virgil
as well as Dante and Petrarch.[42] He enjoyed poetry which contained
colour to please the eye and music which could be 'relished by the most
uncultivated ear'. Roscoe was not himself musical but was interested in
the relationship between music, poetry and painting. There follows in
Roscoe's Life of Lorenzo a review of Lorenzo's more mature poetic
writing, including lyrics, sonnets, devotional poems, hunting songs, love
songs and burlesque. Roscoe described him as the 'restorer of the lyric
poetry of Italy, the promoter of the dramatic, the founder of the satiric,

---

41 Life of Lorenzo by Wm. Roscoe, page 179.

42 Life of Lorenzo - Wm. Roscoe, page 178.

rustic and other forms of composition.'[43] Roscoe seems to support Pico della Mirandola in his expressed opinion that the 'writings of Lorenzo unite the vigour of thought of Dante with the harmony and polish of Petrarch,[44] thus even suggesting that Lorenzo was superior to the great masters of Tuscan poetry. This opinion was not held by many later critics.

Roscoe asserted that Lorenzo 'is not merely entitled to the rank of a poet, but may justly be placed among the distinguished few, who by native strength have made their way through paths untrodden'. He was a great believer in 'native strength' stressing the fact that, for many of his accomplishments, Lorenzo 'was not indebted to a preceptor and that his exquisite taste in poetry, which enabled him to do so much, was an endowment of nature, the want of which no education can supply.'

Roscoe, conscious of his own lack of formal education felt greatly encouraged. In his 'Life of Lorenzo' Roscoe never informs us, as does Guicciardini, 'that Lorenzo desired glory and success more than any man and that even in poetry, in games and other pursuits, he would not permit any to imitate or compete with him and was angry with those who did so.'[45] Roscoe was not a puritan and does not take too seriously the licentiousness of Lorenzo's 'Canzoni a Ballo' - songs written to accompany dancing, a favourite amusement of the populace - telling us solemnly 'that a dance is in fact only a figurative representation of the passion of love, exhibited with more or less delicacy, according to the character and state of civilisation of those who practise it.'[46] One is left wondering whether in the days of his long courtship Roscoe ever took his beloved Jane (Julia in his poems) out to a ball in Liverpool. Certainly Lorenzo, 'the arbiter of the politics of Italy', was only too happy to join in the fun, 'directing the evolutions of a troop of dancing girls.'[47] This pleased the people of Florence.

---

43   Wm. Roscoe, Life of Lorenzo (Bohn), pp.205, et seq.

44   Wm. Roscoe, Life of Lorenzo (Bohn, pp.205, et seq.

45   Guicciardini, History of Florence, English Translation by Cecil Grayson, 1964, page 10.

46   For Roscoe's 'definition' of dancing see his Life of Lorenzo (Bohn), page 204.

47   William Roscoe, Life of Lorenzo (Bohn), page 205.

Many of Roscoe's admirers, perhaps more interested in Italian painting and the arts than in Italian history, must have found chapter IX, which deals with the progress of the arts and the encouragement given by the Medici to artists, sculptors and architects, as full of interest but tantalisingly short. Roscoe relied largely on Vasari (1511-1574) for information regarding the many artists, whom Lorenzo took under his wing. Vasari has for long been regarded as the most important source on Italian Renaissance art. Roscoe quotes Vasari as having said, 'It is highly deserving of notice that all those who studied in the gardens of Medici, and were favoured by Lorenzo, became most excellent artists, which can only be attributed to the exquisite judgement of this great patron of their studies, who could not only distinguish men of genius, but had the will and the power to reward them.' The gardens of Medici, adjacent to the priory of S. Marco, were established by Lorenzo as an art school, where indoors and outside statues, busts and other exhibits were displayed and studied. Bertoldo a favourite pupil of Donatello was appointed superintendent.[48] These gardens were described by Vasari as 'the nursery of men of genius,'[49] the most outstanding of whom was Michelangelo, who was treated as one of the family. Roscoe comments on the fact that in the palace of the Medici at table 'by a commendable regulation the troublesome distinctions of rank were abolished and every person took his place in the order of his arrival.'[50] Michelangelo was one only of many favoured by Lorenzo. In fact they appear to have been as thick as thieves. On one occasion when Michelangelo had completed a beautiful statue in marble, Lorenzo suggested it be buried underground for some time, later unearthed, and be sold as a genuine example of statuary from the ancient world. This was done, but the work was soon found to be a forgery by the purchaser and duly returned. Roscoe reports this incident, but does not comment on the integrity of Lorenzo and Michelangelo who together planned this trickery.[51] Roscoe was a great believer in setting up local academies of art comparable with the Royal Academy founded in London in 1768. There was a considerable difference between the Gardens of Medici and the eighteenth century academy of art. The former resembled a museum with studios, where promising artists worked,

---

48　William Roscoe, Life of Lorenzo, page 312.

49　Vasari Ragionamenti, page 75.

50　Condivi, Vita di Michelagnolo, p.5 et seq.

51　Wm. Roscoe, Life of Leo, page 316.

patronised and financed by Lorenzo out of state funds. The latter were places where public exhibitions were held and formal lectures given. Roscoe, in describing the former, tended to think of the latter.

The final chapter begins with Lorenzo's expressed intention to retire at the age of forty-three, quoted by Fabroni, 'What can be more desirable to a well-regulated mind than the enjoyment of leisure with dignity? This is what all good men wish to obtain, but which great men alone accomplish. Having obtained the object of my cares, I trust I may be allowed to enjoy the sweets of leisure, to share the reputation of my fellow-citizens and to exult in the glory of my native place.'[52] Not long after, Lorenzo told his faithful friend and tutor of his two sons, Poliziano, in the privacy of his bedroom 'that he meant to withdraw himself as much as possible from the tumult of the city, and to devote the remainder of his days to the society of his learned friends.'[53] Lorenzo did not live to enjoy the relaxation and happiness he hoped for. No sooner had Roscoe successfully published his Life of Lorenzo than he also made up his mind to retire at the same age as his hero and for precisely the same reasons. Though Roscoe lived on for many years, he too was not destined to enjoy the relaxation and happiness he was hoping for at such an early stage in his life.

There follows an account of Lorenzo's illness and a dignified and emotional description of his last days and deathbed scene in his villa at Careggi, in the company of his closest friends Pico della Mirandola and Poliziano, who shortly afterwards wrote, 'To judge from Lorenzo's conduct, you would have thought it was they who momentarily expected that fate, from which he appeared to be exempt.'[54]

Lorenzo's fatherly advice to his son and successor, Piero, which was quickly forgotten, is quoted by Roscoe.[55] Evidently Lorenzo died a model death, preserving his good humour to the end even when his bête noir, 'the haughty and enthusiastic' Savonarola appeared on the scene to give him the last rites.[56] Lorenzo became reconciled to God with cheerfulness and to Savonarola with no trace of resentment. Roscoe does not mention the probably apocryphal, and if so scurrilous, account of the scene to the effect that 'the priest's price of salvation included the

52 Fabroni in Vita Laur, i, 196.

53 Wm. Roscoe - Life of Lorenzo, p.326.

54 Wm. Roscoe - Life of Lorenzo, page 330.

55 Wm. Roscoe - Life of Lorenzo, page 328.

56 Wm. Roscoe - Life of Lorenzo, page 329.

restoration of all ill-gotten gains and the restitution of liberty to Florence: to the first Lorenzo agreed, but died unabsolved before he could consent to the second."[57] Nothing is ever mentioned in Roscoe's 'Life of Lorenzo' which might tarnish the blameless character of his hero.

It is difficult to imagine a more inconsequential ending to an otherwise serious book than the last pages of the Life of Lorenzo, which consist of speculation about two mysterious deaths, which occurred soon after Lorenzo's demise, and a bewildering account of events leading to the collapse of the Republic of Florence. The first is the death of Piero, Lorenzo's doctor, who had been so unsuccessful in the diagnosis and treatment of his patient's sickness. Piero's body was found at the bottom of a well shortly after Lorenzo's death. It may have been suicide or perhaps murder. At least the doctor could not have been blamed for the final collapse of Lorenzo caused, as it appears, by another doctor's prescription consisting of pulverised pearls and precious stones mixed with expensive potions.[58] Four different explanations were given for Poliziano's untimely death, the most plausible being that he was killed as a result of a fall from the stairs, as he was singing to his lute an elegy, which he had composed on the death of Lorenzo. Certainly the monody, composed by Poliziano and incorporated by Roscoe into his last chapter complete with his own translation into English, is indicative of 'his anguish and state of mind.'[59] It is unfortunate that a biography which contains a number of excellent chapters and much useful information, should end on so low a key.

Roscoe entrusted the printing of his 'Life of Lorenzo' to Mr. McCreery, 'who by his advice had lately established a press in Liverpool.[60] Although the two volumes were dated and printed in 1795, the book was published in February 1796 by Edwards of Pall Mall. Henry Roscoe remarked that 'the typographical beauty of the first edition attested the skill of McCreery's professional ability.'[61] The first edition was printed at

---

57   Christopher Hibbert - The Rise and Fall of the House of Medici, page 173.

58   Wm. Roscoe, Life of Lorenzo, p.327 (Bohn Edition).

59   Wm. Roscoe, Life of Lorenzo, pages 341, 342 (Bohn Edition).

60   Life of Wm. Roscoe by his son, Henry, Vol.1, page 152.

     - Roscoe and McCreery were kindred spirits. McCreery possessed considerable poetic powers and was devoted to the cause of truth, freedom and human improvement. A few months after Roscoe's death, McCreery and his daughter set out on a journey to Switzerland in the autumn of 1831 . In Paris McCreery fell a victim to cholera and died within two days. Perhaps Roscoe had reason never to venture abroad!

61   Life of Wm. Roscoe by his son, Henry, Vol.1, p.151 and 152.

at Roscoe's expense. All editions in English contained an appendix made up of documents in Latin and Italian, used as resource materials by the author, and a collection of original poems by Lorenzo himself, found in Florence in manuscript and never previously printed. Roscoe was so delighted with these treasures that he arranged for a small selection of the poems to be printed in 1791 as personal gifts for William Clarke and a few of his close literary friends.[62]

Soon after publication of the first edition, Roscoe received letters of appreciation and congratulation from admirers and friends including Lord Orford (Horace Walpole), the Marquis of Lansdowne and Lord Bristol. Roscoe himself liberal and Whig in outlook, was pleasantly surprised to find his work highly commended by the author of the 'Pursuits of Literature', a publication well-known for its Tory sympathies. The writer prefaced his review with the following poetic effusion:

> 'But hark, what solemn strains from Arno's vales
>
> Breathe raptures wafted on the Tuscan gales!
>
> LORENZO rears again his awful head,
>
> And feels his ancient glories round him spread;
>
> The Muses starting from their trance revive,
>
> And at their ROSCOE'S bidding wake and live'.[63]

He continued: 'See the Life of Lorenzo de Medici called the Magnificent, by William Roscoe.' I cannot but congratulate the public upon this great and important addition to classical history, which I regard as a phenomenon in literature in every point of view. It is pleasant to consider a gentleman, not under the auspices of a university, nor beneath the shade of academic bowers, but in the practice of the law, and business of great extent, and resident in the remote commercial town of Liverpool, where nothing is heard of but Guinea ships, slaves, blacks and merchandise, investigating and describing the rise and progress of every polite art in Italy, at the revival of learning, with acuteness, depth and precision with the spirit of the poet and the solidity of the historian. For my own part I have not terms sufficient to express my admiration of his genius and erudition, or of my gratitude for the amusement and information I have received.'

---

62 Life of Wm. Roscoe by his son, Henry, Vol.1, p.151 and 152.

63 Life of William Roscoe by his son, Henry, Vol.1, page 168 et seq.

Roscoe sold the copyright of the first edition of his Life of Lorenzo to Cadell and Davies, a London publisher for the sum of £1,200. Aware of the need for careful correction, he wrote to Cadell and Davies on June 24, 1796 referring to the second edition due to be published later that year:-[64] "I intended long ago to have transmitted you the corrected copy of Lorenzo de'Medici, but have been prevented partly by frequent and unavoidable absences from home. It is now however nearly ready and it shall be sent off very soon, as I would by no means have the new edition to be deprived of these corrections. I have also thoughts of pre-fixing to the October edition an additional preface or advertisement of some length which I have nearly prepared for the purpose of returning my acknowledgements to my friends and for replying to some objections both at home and abroad." The second edition duly appeared, corrected and in two volumes, in the autumn of 1796.

One of many commendations came from a complete stranger, Dr Parr a history don at Brasenose College Oxford, who introduced himself to Roscoe, informing him that the contents of his book surpassed his expectation.[65] 'You have thrown', he said, the clearest and fullest light upon a period most interesting to every scholar. You have produced much that was unknown, and to that which was known, you have given perspicuity and grace.' He went on to say, 'I will with your permission, send you a list of mistakes which I have found in some Latin passages ... I shall proceed further in pointing out one or two expressions which seem capable of improvement and in stating my reasons for dissenting from you upon a very few facts of very little importance.'

Roscoe acknowledged receipt of Parr's friendly letter and expressed the readiness and satisfaction with which he was prepared to receive the promised criticisms. Shortly afterwards Parr dispatched a letter, dated December 27, 1797, enclosing his list of suggested corrections.[66] He told Roscoe that the edition he had before him was that of 1796, which he had borrowed from the librarian of New College. The letter and the accompanying list might well have cast a shadow on the festive season. Replying on December 28, 1797 Roscoe admitted that the letter and its

---

64   Manuscript of signed letter, Hornby Library (Picton Library) Liverpool, from Wm. Roscoe to Cadell and Davies.

65   Life of W.M., Vol.1, page 180 at seq.

66   Roscoe Papers 2881.

contents had taken him by surprise. He wrote explaining that the length of the list of corrections and observations alarmed and surprised him, suggesting that his mistakes were innumerable.[67] The task of tidying up the 'Life of Lorenzo' Roscoe compared to the cleansing of an Augean stable and he was relieved that it had not exhausted Parr's patience. Roscoe could see that Parr's criticisms fell into three categories - mistakes in the Latin quotations, a few parts of the English narrative capable of improvement and disagreement upon matters of minor importance. In answer to Dr. Parr's criticism of his punctuation, (presumably of the Latin texts), Roscoe pointed out that before 1500, the only punctuation mark was the colon, and that Aldus was the first printer to use the comma. Roscoe agreed to look again at 'the exaggerated metaphors' he had used in his description of Savonarola and his preaching'. He continued 'And now my dear sir, l will release you from the additional fatigue of reading this letter'. He admitted his inability to write Latin and concluded by saying, 'I am happy to find that my errors are not either so numerous or so important.'[68]

A comparison of the fourth and subsequent editions of the 'Life of Lorenzo' with the 1796 edition indicates that corrections of the Latin texts were attended to in the third edition of 1799; also that some attention was paid to improving the author's English in places and that nothing was done about differences of opinion. Dr Parr may have been responsible for an alteration in the very last sentence of the book, in which Roscoe wrote of the collapse of the Republic of Florence under the Medici.

The clumsy revised version reads - 'the desire for information fortunately terminates when the materials for supplying it are not to be found.'[69] This is far less elegant than Roscoe's original:- 'the desire for information... terminates, where the want of it begins.'

A further four editions in English (seven in all) were published during Roscoe's life-time, two before and two after the publication in 1822 of his robust defence of 'the Life of Lorenzo' entitled 'Illustrations Historical and Critical of the Life of Lorenzo de'Medici called the Magnificent.' The publication of this latter work evidently revived interest in his biography of Lorenzo. After Roscoe's death four further editions, revised

---

67 Roscoe Papers 2883 and Life of W.R., Vol.1, page 183.

68 Roscoe Papers 2883.

69 Life of Lorenzo de' Medici, Wm. Roscoe, page 370, Bohn Edition.

by his son Thomas, were published in 1846, 1847, 1851 and 1865. Another edition, with a memoir of the author and edited by William Hazlitt, the essayist, was published in 1883, eighty-seven years after the publication of the first edition. This is remarkable testimony to the popularity in Britain of Roscoe's 'Life of Lorenzo' - an achievement attained by few biographers or historians.

An edition of Roscoe's 'Life of Lorenzo' was printed and published in America in 1803 by Messrs Bronson and Chauncey in Philadelphia. The knowledge that his work had reached a new continent and was so much appreciated gave the author immense satisfaction 'heightened by the consideration that this is the sentiment of a country where political, civil and religious liberty are enjoyed in a degree almost unexampled in the history of the human race'.[70]

The first foreign translations of Roscoe's Life of Lorenzo were published in Germany in 1797. The translators were Dr Forster, a scientist and botanist, who accompanied Captain Cook on his voyage round the world, and Kurt Sprengel, writer of 'the Authentic History of Medicine', both professors at the University of Halle in Germany.[71] Sprengel in the introduction to his translation explained that 'he does not wish to debar the lovers of Italian literature of those beautiful poems of Lorenzo, which Roscoe for the first time printed.'[72] These were therefore included in the edition. On grounds of expense he decided not to include Roscoe's appendix of Latin and Italian documents. There followed a translation by François Thurot into French, published in Paris in 1799, a second edition appearing in London in 1800. A translation of Roscoe's Life of Lorenzo into Italian by Gaetano Mecherini, at the request of Fabroni, was published in Pisa in 1799 and again in 1816. Finally a translation into Greek was made by X.A. Parmenidas, which included a life of the author abridged from the English of Henry Roscoe's biography of his father. This was published in Athens in 1858.

---

70 Letter to the Publishers Bronson and Chauncey, 1803, from William Roscoe, quoted in Life of Wm. Roscoe by his son, Henry, Vol.1, p.201.

71 Life of Dr Currie, vol. ii, page 95 - from a letter of Dr. Currie to a medical friend in America.

72 William Roscoe, Illustrations, Historical and Critical of the Life of Lorenzo, Appendix page 19.

The most searching criticism of Roscoe's Life of Lorenzo came not from English readers, but from French, German and Italian scholars. Sprengel, in dedicating to his brother his German translation of Roscoe's 'Life of Lorenzo', explained that he had first intended to make a translation of Fabroni's work, but had changed his mind after studying Roscoe's biography.[73] He found 'the Italian was hesitating and partial in his judgement and that he wanted (lacked) the spirit of free discussion and extensive knowledge of the Englishman'. Roscoe was delighted with 'the beautiful parallel between the character of Lorenzo and that of Pericles: of the golden age of Florence with that of Athens' drawn by Sprengel in his dedication.[74] In an effusive letter of thanks, Roscoe spoke warmly of the bond of union which had grown up between himself, 'a stranger living in a remote part of the world' and Sprengel, arising out of their shared experience of similar emotions in the contemplation of the character of the great man, Lorenzo de'Medici.[75]

François Thurot introduced his French translation with a letter addressed to Citizen Jean Bartholemi Lecouteulx, in which he claimed to be impressed by Roscoe's liberal ideas and deep research. He admired his candour and the noble manner, 'noble et décente', in which Roscoe discussed the writings of others.[76] Like Roscoe's dilettanti admirers in England, Thurot spoke of Roscoe's elegant good taste and refinement. He then launched out into a searching criticism of the Life of Lorenzo. Roscoe had failed to employ 'une methode assez rigoreuse'. He criticised Roscoe's lack of an overall plan, commenting on the fact that the book is made up of chapters on diverse subjects, loosely connected and at times repetitive. Roscoe was hesitant or afraid to leave out less important or irrelevant parts of his work. Thurot complained that the bibliographical and other notes (fort multipliès) interrupt the flow of his narrative. Finally he arrived at his 'reproche plus grave', which was that he found it difficult to defend Roscoe's excessive partiality for his hero and especially for his failure even to mention or condemn Lorenzo's 'immeasurable ambition' as a tyrant and despotic ruler. Roscoe had failed to identify the cause of Lorenzo's weakness and the down-fall of the Medici

---

73 William Roscoe, Illustrations of the Life of Lorenzo Appendix No. 1, page 18.

74 William Roscoe, Illustrations of the Life of Lorenzo, Appendix No.1 and Life of Wm. Roscoe by his son, Henry, Vol.1, page 198.

75 Life of Wm. Roscoe by his son Henry, Vol.1, p.199.

76 Wm. Roscoe, Illustrations of the Life of Lorenzo, Appendix II, pp.23 et seq.

Medici - the scandalous system of hereditary rule, an institution he regarded as inconsistent with a free society. Thurot reckoned that Roscoe as an Englishman, living in a country not yet liberated, and accustomed to a monarchy and an unchallenged establishment based on hereditary power, would never think of criticising or condemning the powers that be in Florence.[77]

Soon after the publication of his Life of Lorenzo, Roscoe's attention was drawn to a new work in Italian, by the Abate Andres, entitled 'On the Origin, Progress and Present State of every branch of Literature'. The author, a Spanish Jesuit, was considered to be the best literary historian in Italy since the death of Tiraboschi of Modena in 1794. In this book Andres, after a general commendation of Roscoe's Life of Lorenzo, proceeded to criticise the work 'on the ground that it was inadequate as a history of the revival of letters and science in the fifteenth century.'[78] Roscoe, defending himself against this charge, asserted that he neither had the qualifications nor the knowledge to write such a history. His Life of Lorenzo was intended to be the biography of an individual and he had deliberately confined himself to such subjects which seemed to illustrate Lorenzo's character.

Andres also took Roscoe to task for 'deviating from the path of historical impartiality' by misrepresenting an important fact relating to the conduct of Pope Sixtus IV in the conspiracy of the Pazzi.[79] The important fact stated by Roscoe was simply that Pope Sixtus IV was known to have been an accomplice in the plot to overthrow the Florentine government of the Medici, which resulted in the murder of Lorenzo's brother, Giuliano, and in Lorenzo's escape from assassination. Roscoe believed the evidence of Pope Sixtus' complicity to be 'too explicit to be misunderstood and too strong to be confuted.'[80] He was even able to incorporate in his 'Illustrations of the Life of Lorenzo' the copy of a document, which came to light after the publication of his Life of Lorenzo, discovered in the Archivio delle Riformagioni at Florence.[81] The document consists of a letter from Pope Sixtus, in which he attempts to

---

77 Wm. Roscoe, Illustrations of the Life of Lorenzo', Appendix No.2, page 26.

78 Wm. Roscoe, 'Illustrations of the Life of Lorenzo' pages 11 and 12.

79 Wm. Roscoe, 'Illustraitons of the Life of Lorenzo' page 13.

80 Wm. Roscoe, Illustrations of Life of Lorenzo, Preface page 13.

81 Lettre Inédite De La Seigneurie de Florence au Pape Sixte iv, 21 Juillet, 1478, to be found in the Appendix, no.5 of Roscoe's Illustrations of the Life of Lorenzo.

prevail upon the people of Florence to expel Lorenzo from the city as a tyrant and an enemy of the common interests of Christendom. This incriminating document and the appendix of which it forms a part were omitted from the Italian translation of Roscoe's Illustrations of the Life of Lorenzo.[82]

Roscoe, during the years following the publication of his Life of Lorenzo in 1796, must often have felt sorely tempted openly to challenge those of his critics who accused him of misrepresenting the character and exaggerating the achievements of Lorenzo. This he wisely refrained from doing until, years later, he discovered references to his biography in a work entitled 'Histoire des Republiques Italiennes du Moyen Age', written by a celebrated French historian, M. de Sismondi, and published in Paris between 1809 and 1818. In the eleventh volume of this history de Sismondi wrote 'Could one have supposed that at the end of three hundred years, at a distance of three hundred leagues, the author of the Life of Lorenzo de' Medici would have employed his talents in deceiving himself and others as to the importance, the claims and virtues of his hero?'[83] In the same volume de Sismondi lost no opportunity of attacking Lorenzo, contending that 'his public measures were always injurious to the liberties of his country; that he corrupted his fellow-citizens by ostentatious and expensive spectacles; that he incurred the resentment of his countrymen by his tyrannical measures; that the conspiracy of the Pazzi was a struggle for liberty, justifiable in the circumstances under which it took place; that by his political conduct he diminished the importance of Florence in the affairs of Italy, that he, so far from being the great character represented, is not to be placed in the rank of great man, or even to be considered a superior person in poetry or in art.'[84] He also accused Roscoe

---

82 This translation by Signor V. Pecciolini, at the request of Roscoe's correspondent, Canonico Moreno, was published in Florence in 1823 in two volumes. Life of Wm. Roscoe by his son Henry, Vol.2, page 275.

83 J.C.L. Simonde de Sismondi, Histoire des Republiques Italiennes. Tom. XI, p.85 1809-1818.

84 De Sismondi, Histoire des Republiques Italiennes Tom XI page 6 et seq. This ill accords with the pronouncement of a great historian, Machiavelli, closer by far in time and space, who made this pronouncement: - 'Of Fortune and of God Lorenzo was supremely loved, wherefore all his enterprises ended well and those of his enemies ill ... All the citizens mourned his death and all the princes of Italy ... and that they had good reason to grieve the result soon showed ... As soon as Lorenzo died, all those bad seeds began to sprout which not long after, he who could quell them no longer alive, ruined and are still ruining Italy'. Machiavelli, Florentine History, 1520.

of 'exalting the services of the Medici family, glossing over their crimes and dissimulating or concealing the independent and resentful spirit of the Florentines etc.' These reflections on Lorenzo and himself stung Roscoe to the quick. He believed it to be wrong 'to suffer the memory of Lorenzo to rest without a further vindication... I cannot remain in silent indifference, and suffer it to be defaced by the hands of prejudice and malice, or insulted by the attacks of malice and spleen: I have, therefore, endeavoured to secure it by an additional defence, which may keep at a distance the rude feet that would trample on his ashes, and may secure my own labours against similar attacks.'[85]

A copy of Roscoe's 'Illustrations of the Life of Lorenzo' was sent soon after its publication in 1822 to M. de Sismondi, who acknowledged receipt in a letter from Geneva dated July 2, 1824. De Sismondi had been astonished and flattered to receive Roscoe's defence in book form, but remained unconvinced, persisting in his opinion of Lorenzo. Roscoe replied expressing regret that his literary effort had failed in its purpose.[86] Though de Sismondi and Roscoe begged to disagree on the subject of Lorenzo, they continued on the friendliest terms. During a visit to Liverpool not long after, de Sismondi was the guest of Roscoe for several days. Roscoe's son, Henry, tells us that the two literary contraversialists found great pleasure in each other's company.[87] It may be that Roscoe's idolisation of his hero led the Frenchman to take the part of the devil's advocate and overstate his case. Roscoe believed that de Sismondi's doctrinaire political views, it being the time of the French revolution, had obscured and distorted his perception of Lorenzo and Florence under the Medici. Roscoe was not impressed by de Sismondi's failure to substantiate from early records and contemporary histories his personal view of Lorenzo. De Sismondi was prepared to countenance violence and bloodshed as a means of effecting political change, a view which was totally abhorrent to Roscoe.

The success of Roscoe's 'Life of Lorenzo' shows that the author met a very real need. Believing that Lorenzo had not received the recognition he deserved, Roscoe wrote because he wanted to share his interest in

---

85 William Roscoe, Illustrations, Historical & Critical, of the Life of Lorenzo - Prefatory Observations, page 43.

86 Life of Wm. Roscoe by his son Henry, Vol.2, p.280.

87 Life of Wm. Roscoe by his son Henry, Vol.2, p.282.

Lorenzo and his enthusiasm for Renaissance Florence with his fellow countrymen. To suggest, as for example Roy Porter does, that Roscoe 'wrote to highlight the parallel as he saw it, between Renaissance Florence and modern Britain,'[88] is somewhat misleading as it is only partially true. Any careful reader of the 'Life of Lorenzo' will discover few explicit comparisons between eighteenth century Britain and Florence under the Medici. It is doubtful whether Roscoe had any axe to grind other than the purpose he stated simply in his preface.[89] The book is aptly described as a 'Kulturgeschichte' of the Renaissance era by C.P. Darcy, who reminds us that Roscoe conceived of the whole cultural revival in Italy as centering on the Medici family's intelligent direction and liberal patronage.[90] It is more than likely that Roscoe in the course of writing, and his readers, on further reflection, began to see some resemblance between the eighteenth century blossoming of the arts in Liverpool and elsewhere in England and the cultural Renaissance in Italy. It must also have become evident that in some respects, but emphatically not in others, there was a faint similarity between the role of Lorenzo in Florence and Roscoe's role as promoter of the arts in Liverpool. Some of their experiences and achievements as well as their ideals were similar, but in character they were poles apart. Roscoe, despite his failure in business leading to bankruptcy, enjoyed a long and fairly tranquil life, whereas Lorenzo lived life to the full, dying at the age of forty-three, having suffered many traumatic experiences.

Roscoe endued with a strong and lofty sense of duty and moral purpose, believed that lessons are to be learnt from past history, and did not hesitate to adopt a somewhat didactic and moralistic stance, which many of his critics have found irritating. His image of Florence as an ideal city was not altogether realistic. He was familiar with Guicciardini's History of Florence, which describes the city as it was at the time of Lorenzo thus:-[91]

'The city enjoyed perfect peace, the citizens were united in perfect harmony, and the government so powerful that no one dared oppose it. The people every day delighted in shows, revelries and other novelties; they were fed, as the city was supplied with victuals, and all its activities

---

88 Roy Porter, English Society in the Eighteenth Century, 1982, page 242.

89 William Roscoe, Life of Lorenzo, preface page 18.

90 C.P. Darcy, 'Encouragement of the Fine Arts in Lancashire', Manchester University Press, 1976, page 35.

91 Francesco Guicciardini, History of Florence, English Translation by C. Grayson, 1964.

flourished. Men of intellect and ability were contented; for all letters, all arts, all talents were welcomed and recognised.'

This delightful state of affairs greatly appealed to Roscoe, and yet he would much have preferred to have seen the whole community, and not the intelligentsia only, developing an interest in art. Roscoe was not merely interested in supporting artists; he was equally anxious to help working people develop a taste for art, not forgetting that it was a friendly painter and engraver, employed at a chinaware factory next to his home on Mount Pleasant, who kindled his interest in the arts as a boy.

Roscoe, despite the fact that he was a high-minded Unitarian bent on improvement moral and social, was human and realistic enough to tell in detail and with relish many stories of the extraordinary behaviour, gossip and scandal of the city of Florence. He overlooked the weaknesses, the licentiousness and the excesses of many characters about whom he wrote.

It is probably true to say that we learn as much, if not more, of the character of the author himself as we do of the somewhat illusory and seemingly contradictory character of Lorenzo from the reading of his 'Life of Lorenzo de'Medici, called the Magnificent'. Roscoe performed a useful service to future generations of students by bringing together in one book such a wealth of information about his hero.

Chapter Three

Roscoe's Writings
The Life and Pontificate of Leo X

On more than one occasion in his life Roscoe undertook an arduous and exacting task, not of his own volition, but out of a sense of obligation to his friends, who had gone out of their way to help him. The 'Life of Lorenzo', completed at the height of his professional career as an attorney, was a supreme effort and he was thankful to see his work finished and published in 1796. The book became a 'best seller' and as G.W. Mathews, in his memoir of William Roscoe, tells us: "Like Byron on the publication of 'Childe Harold's Pilgrimage', Roscoe awoke one morning to find himself famous."[1] Among many, who wrote to congratulate him on his achievement, was Lord Bristol, at that time resident in Rome, who had already been in touch with Mr Cadell, the publisher, begging "to know the place of residence of Mr Roscoe, the ingenious, learned and elegant author of the 'Life of Lorenzo de' Medici' - what is his profession - what his connection and what present of books, pictures or statues might be most welcome to him?"[2] On ascertaining Roscoe's address, Lord Bristol wrote a letter congratulating him on his work and a further letter offering him the use of his apartments at Rome or at Naples, a tempting offer wasted on Roscoe, who showed no inclination ever to leave the shores of Britain. Lord Bristol wrote, "In the meantime I venture to exhort you, 'Perge ut incepisti', and take for your next theme a subject still more extensive, still more worthy of your abilities. 'Tis the sequel of Lorenzo that I propose to you, in the life of his son, Leo X. You see at once, Sir, what a glorious, animating era it embraces; and who is so fit to paint the manhood of arts, of science and religious information, as the

---

1. William Roscoe - a Memoir by Godfrey W. Mathews, published for the Centenary in London 1931 - page 26.
2   Life of W.R. Vol.1, pages 162 et seq.

happy and elegant writer who has so satisfactorily sketched and delineated their infancy?"[3]

Roscoe received this suggestion with mixed feelings. One might suppose he wanted to retire to write and devote the rest of his life to literary, artistic and horticultural pursuits. At the same time he was fully aware of his responsibility to his large family. He had become deeply involved in the campaign for the abolition of the slave trade and other political activities. He may have felt obliged not to disappoint his friends, but appears to have been only too happy to accede to the request for a sequel to his Life of Lorenzo in the form of a biography of Lorenzo's son, Giovanni, who became Pope Leo X. The fact that Fabroni set to work on a Life of Leo X soon after publication of his Life of Lorenzo (of which Roscoe made full use) might well have been an added incentive for Roscoe to do the same in English.

In his preface to the Life and Pontificate of Leo X, Roscoe explained in greater detail his reasons for launching out on this project.[4] First his Life of Lorenzo had opened the way to a variety of researches connected with the events of the ensuing period. His work on Lorenzo 'was considered by many, not unjustly, as only the vestibule to a more spacious building, which it was incumbent on the author at some period to complete'. Roscoe had become so deeply immersed in the literature and history of the period and had been supplied with so much help in his researches by friends at home and abroad, some of whom provided him with original documents, that he felt obliged to go forward. Secondly, there was no historical work in English covering Pope Leo X and his tenure of office. Roscoe explained that 'the elegant and pathetic poet, William Collins, was said to have planned in the mid-eighteenth century

---

3   The eighteenth century Earl, Lord Bristol, through royal patronage and family connections, had been appointed Bishop of Derry. Adam Nicolson, in the Times Magazine, Feb. 19. 1994, says of Lord Bristol, the Earl Bishop - 'If he was unspeakably mean to his family, his love of display and his thirst for applause meant that he could always be extravagant with friends'. This accords well with his two letters to Roscoe (1797), who was wise to refuse Lord Bristol's offer of a flat in Rome, or at Naples, or of books or even of a statue! Roscoe would have been familiar with Virgil's dictum - 'Timeo Danaos et done ferentes'. The Bishop may well have been an admirer of Pope Leo X, but he died in 1803, two years before publication of the biography he urged Roscoe to write.

4   Life and Pontificate of Leo X, Wm. Roscoe Preface page V, Vl et seq.

5   Life of Leo X, William Roscoe, Preface page X.

Pope Leo (1513-21) excommunicated Luther in 1521.
Attributed to Sebastiano del Piombo.

to write a Life of Leo X, which was to include a history of the revival of literature, learning and the arts during his time.[5] Among Collins' friends were Dr Johnson and two brothers, Joseph and Thomas Warton, all of whom shared a common interest in this period. Roscoe quoted Dr Johnson as having said 'I have heard him (Collins) speak with great kindness of Leo X and with great resentment of his tasteless successor, but probably not a page of the history was ever written.'[6] Joseph Warton a contemporary of Collins at Winchester and Oxford, in his 'Essay on the Life and Writings of Pope' spoke of the encouragement given to literature and the fine arts by Leo X, mentioning that a friend of his (presumably Collins) is engaged in writing 'the History of the Age of Leo X.'[7] Collins died at the age of 39, the very year Warton's 'Essay' was published (1759). Nearly forty years later in 1797 Roscoe had the pleasure of meeting Dr Joseph Warton, who told him that he and his brother, Thomas, and other friends had planned to write 'a history of the revival of letters not only in Italy, but in all the principal countries of Europe.'[8] This ambitious project came to nothing 'for want of public encouragement'. Thus the self-educated Roscoe stepped in where angels feared (or were too lazy) to tread and set about the task of writing a history of Leo X and his times in the English language, spurred on by the knowledge that there was a demand for such a work. Roscoe would have been wiser to collaborate with others than to undertake this daunting task without help or guidance. Having made up his mind to go forward with his 'Life of and Pontificate of Leo X', Roscoe set to work in the autumn of 1798, busily collecting information and resource material. He was already familiar with the earliest history of Leo, written by Paolo Giovio in Latin, translated into Italian and published in Florence in 1549.[9] He acknowledged that the work "contained much authentic information and was less satirical in spirit than Giovio's other writings". He was also acquainted with the histories of Guicciardini and the writings of Muratori. He also had the benefit of A. Fabroni's Leonis Pontificis Maximi Vita, published in Pisa in 1797 only a year before he himself engaged in the same task. In a letter to Lord Bristol he stated that he

---

6   Life of Leo X, William Roscoe, Preface page X.

7   Essay on Pope 1756 Joseph Warton - See Life of William Roscoe by his son, Henry Vol. 1, pages 303 and 304 and footnote.

8   Life of W.R. Vol.1, p.304.

9   Life of Leo X, William Roscoe, Preface page IX.

10 Life of W.R., Vol. 1, p.306.

could not be satisfied with retailing among his countrymen a compound elaborated from the works of Giovio, Muratori and Guicciardini.[10] He felt them to be inadequate, because they contained insufficient information relating to the political, artistic and literary history of the period. Once again Roscoe was fortunate in securing help in collecting books, manuscripts and copies of contemporary documents from Florence, Rome, Venice and Paris. He evidently experienced difficulty at the outset in planning the purpose and scope of the book. In an unpublished tract mentioned by his son Henry, written after the publication of his Life of Leo, Roscoe said he considered it to be a sort of continuation of his former history of the Life of Lorenzo de' Medici. He felt impelled 'to include an account of events of the greatest curiosity and importance in history, which took place between the death of Lorenzo and the election of Leo.'[11] The more he read the more he became immersed in the history of the period, and later he acknowledged that his intention had become, as far as the subject would allow, to embrace the history of the principal events in Europe from the downfall of Constantinople in 1453 to the accession of Charles V, thus connecting, though by links of very inferior workmanship, the golden histories of Gibbon and Robertson.'[12] The scope of Roscoe's book became increasingly ambitious. William Robertson, Principal of Edinburgh University published a History of Charles V in 1769 which brought him an European reputation as well as a large sum of £4,500. Roscoe conceived the idea of bridging the gap between the end of Gibbon's monumental work, the Decline and Fall of the Roman Empire, and the beginning of Robertson's highly successful work. Conscious as Roscoe evidently was, of his inexperience as a historian, he would have been wiser, at an early stage, to have sought advice and guidance in regard to the composition of what was originally intended to be an account of Leo X's life and pontificate.

The first substantial help in gathering resource materials came from Lord Holland. Permission was obtained from the Grand Duke of Tuscany by Lord Holland for Mr Penrose, 'the British Resident' in Florence, to supervise the copying of a large number of letters and papers which formed two folio volumes, each containing over three hundred pages, illustrating the early life of Pope Leo X.[13] Roscoe received these with

---

11 Life of W.R. Vol.1 page 302 there appears to be no trace of the tract now.
12 Life of W.R. Vol.1, p.321.
13 Life of W.R. Vol.1, p.312.

great satisfaction and was able to make full use of them, though sadly there is no trace of them today. He was also anxious to procure as much information as possible from the Vatican archives in Rome. This he was unable to obtain because on account of political uncertainty in Europe and for reasons of strict security, they were regarded as 'Secret Archives' and not available for public scrutiny. However when Roscoe had almost given up hope, he received an offer of assistance from a certain Mr John Johnson, a gentleman who had been travelling in Italy, who had been told by Canonico Bandini, at that time in charge of the Laurentian library in Florence, that Roscoe was engaged in writing a life of Leo X.[14] Johnson claimed to be acquainted with Cardinal Borgia, the Abbate Marini, Prefetto dell' Archivio Vaticano and others likely to be willing to help with materials for Roscoe's work. Johnson asked Roscoe to give 'precise details respecting any particular documents which he wished to be examined.'

Roscoe wrote an appreciative but guarded reply. After explaining that he had almost completed the first volume of his work, he stated that he had received all the information he required from Florence, and that, if necessary he could himself communicate directly with Canonico Bandini and the Abbate Fontani. What he really wanted most urgently was information from the archives in Rome about Leo X's immediate predecessors, Alexander VI and Julius II and after that further information about Pope Leo X himself. There was a lack of precision in respect of the particular documents Roscoe wanted to see and Mr Johnson was clearly expected to use his own judgement in the choice of materials to be copied for forwarding. Roscoe had written rather vaguely - 'with respect of Leo X, everything that refers to it will be of importance to me, whether it concerns political transactions and negotiations, his encouragement of literature and art, his conduct both in public and private life: in short whatever has any connection with his history or with any branch of his family. I find that anecdotes and circumstances, trivial and unimportant in themselves, often acquire value from comparison with other parts of a person's character and conduct; and I wish to collect all I can respecting this pontiff, in order to appreciate so far as is within my power, his very extraordinary and equivocal character.'[15]

---

14   Life of W.R. Vol.1, page 311 et seq.
15   Life of W.R. Vol.1, page 313 et seq.

Mr Johnson's offer of help was most opportune. He was able to collect manuscripts and copies of manuscripts in Rome, one of which was the fragment of an unpublished Life of Leo X, written in Latin, describing events up to the year 1516.[16] He was able to procure printed books as well as valuable tracts only available in Rome. On his return from Rome to England, Johnson visited Venice, where he was given by the librarian of St. Marco, the Abbate Morelli, a list of books and documents likely to be of use for a biography of Leo X. This led to a correspondence between Morelli and Roscoe which proved invaluable.[17] Roscoe was able to make use of diaries kept by two consecutive Masters of Ceremonies in the Pope's chapel during the time of Leo X and his two immediate predecessors, Alexander VI and Julius II. The first of these was Giovanni Burcado, commonly called Burchard, a native of Strasbourg.[18] The second was Paris de Grassis, a native of Bologna, who succeeded Burchard as Master of Ceremonies. Burchard was appointed to this office during the reign of Pope Sixtus IV, in whose time the diary had been restricted to matters related to his duties in the chapel. However after Pope Sixtus IV's death he broadened the scope of his diary, enriching it with anecdotes and matters not strictly related to his allotted task. Leaks from within a papal or royal household have always made popular reading. According to Roscoe, Burchard's diary was written in Latin 'in a pedestrian and semi-barbarian style, but with an apparent accuracy and minuteness as to facts, which gave it an air of veracity.'[19]

Several later writers, who were interested in the conduct of Pope Alexander V and his son, Caesare Borgia, made full use of it.

Roscoe was anxious to study the Diary of Paris de Grassis, which could only be found in the National Library of Paris. On a visit to France in 1802, his friend, the Rev. W. Shepherd, was able to make a careful study of the diary, and on his return to Liverpool, handed over copies of selected entries, which threw additional light on the history of Leo X and particularly on the circumstances of his death.[20]

---

16 Life of W.R. Vol.1, page 313 et seq.

17 A letter from Morelli is printed in the appendix to Roscoe's 'Illustrations of the Life of Lorenzo de'Medici', number IX. Unfortunately Henry Roscoe fails to give details of the list of resources recommended to his father by Morelli.

18 William Roscoe, Life and Pontificate of Leo X, Preface pages XVIII and XIX.

19 Wm. Roscoe, Preface to his Life of Leo X page XIX.

20 Life of W.R. Vol.1, page 315.

It was in the autumn of 1798, soon after retirement from his practice as a lawyer, that Roscoe started work on his Life and Pontificate of Leo X. His son, Henry, spoke of the unremitting devotion with which his father prosecuted his biographical studies.[21] The complexity of the task he had undertaken and the practical difficulty of weaving the mass of information, supplied to him, into a coherent story, caused him much anxiety and many a sleepless night. He suffered a breakdown in health and was ordered by his doctor to take a complete rest for some months. Roscoe's hopes of a leisurely retirement at Allerton were dashed by the pressure of unforeseen business commitments. Despite all this he persevered and his feelings at this anxious time were well described in a sonnet written when the book was nearing completion.[22] Roscoe, in addressing this moving sonnet to the 'Mighty Spirits of the illustrious Dead', gives us a vivid expression of his feelings at that time. His solitary task involved quitting 'the social circle and the downy bed' and continued 'for many a toilsome day and many a patient year'. He expressed similar sentiments in a letter to his friend, Dr. Smith, in January 1804, by which time he had almost completed two volumes and expressed the hope of publication the following year.

The Life and Pontificate of Leo, which occupied Roscoe's leisure hours for five long years, was published in the summer of 1805 in four weighty volumes by Messrs Cadell and Davies and the first impression of a thousand copies was sold immediately. Roscoe sold half of his copyright in the work to Cadell and Davies for the sum of £2,000.

Roscoe wasted no time in sending copies of the book to his literary friends and to a few distinguished persons to whom he was anxious to show his regard, the first of whom was Thomas Jefferson, President of the United States,who was already in possession of a copy of his Life of Lorenzo.[23] Although Roscoe was happy to receive blandishments from his admirers following the publication of his 'Life and Pontificate of Leo X', he realised his work might not receive universal approval. In a letter to Lord St. Vincent, a few weeks before the book was launched, he wrote, 'a publication on this subject must comprise topics of considerable

---

21 Life of W.R. Vol.1, page 317.

22 George Chandler, William Roscoe of Liverpool, page 451.

23 Life of W.M. Vol.1, page 321.

delicacy, as well in religion as in politics, as in morals and literature; and in other words, must involve questions which have given rise to dissension and persecution in all subsequent times. In the account of the Reformation, I am well aware that my book will give satisfaction neither to the Catholics nor to the Protestants; yet of the two, I apprehend most the displeasure of the latter.'[24]

Roscoe expected his account of the Reformation to attract criticism. What he did not expect was the bombshell launched by the staid and scholarly Edinburgh Review in January 1806, in which his work was severely criticised on other than religious grounds. He was so shaken that he failed to realise that parts of the review were not altogether uncomplimentary. The reviewer paid Roscoe the compliment of taking him seriously enough to incorporate verbatim seven closely printed pages of extracts from the 'Life and Pontificate of Leo X', as well as a lengthy quotation, fifty two lines in all, consisting of a translation in verse by Roscoe of Greek verses prefixed by Musurus to the first edition of Plato by Aldus, verses which seemed out of place in the Life of Leo X and even less relevant in the Edinburgh Review critique. At the end of his review the writer summed up his criticism as follows:-[25]

'Upon the whole, then, these ponderous volumes have disappointed our expectations of obtaining an adequate history of the revival of learning, worthy at least of the importance of the subject. The prevailing defect of the work is a minute and tedious prolixity, and the want of sufficient energy of thought or of style. The accumulation of materials does not always add a proportionable value to history; and an author has learned but half the secrets of his trade who is ignorant of the art of blotting, to which the greatest writers have been indebted for their success. No labour can be too great to attain perfection; and if, instead of endeavouring, in his preface, to extend the defects of his history, Mr Roscoe had transcribed it over again, under the eye of some severe critic, and had resolutely reduced it to half its present size, the remainder from the condensation of the narrative, would have acquired an additional value, when every idle anecdote or superfluous incident was carefully expunged, and the redundance of sentiment or of diction retrenched. As it stands, the history may please the dilettante, to whom the medallion

---

24   Life of W.R. Vol.1. p.330.
25   Edinburgh Review - January 1806, page 357.

and verses are, perhaps, a sufficient recommendation; but it neither will gratify the general reader, nor ought it to supersede any future effort upon the subject, when the present edition has passed away. In general, however, its materials will always be valuable to future historians, by whom the author's opinions, in matters of taste and criticism, will always be respected and his writings impress us with one uniform conviction that he is a truly amiable and benevolent man.'[26] The Edinburgh Review was not the only periodical to pronounce judgement on Roscoe's Life of Leo. Scurrilous attacks were made in the Christian Observer, the Critical Review and The Literary Journal.[27] The Edinburgh Review was the only periodical to take the work seriously.

Roscoe, deeply hurt by the reception accorded by these periodicals to his work, maintained a dignified silence, though he felt obliged to answer the charges of misrepresentation, inaccuracy and bias against Luther in favour of Pope Leo X. What upset him most were those criticisms which reflected on his competence and reputation as an historian. His son and faithful biographer Henry, loyal as always to his father, pointed out that the Life of Leo X 'was never intended to be a history of the revival of learning.'[28] Had it been so, the Edinburgh Review critic might have been justified in declaring it inadequate. Roscoe on a number of occasions had acknowledged this to be a task beyond his powers. The fact is that from the beginning there had been no coherent plan and no clear indication of the scope and purpose of the book. What was intended to be a biography of Leo X became a random collection of essays on all manner of contemporary issues, events and personages. Roscoe was a voracious reader, his interests were numerous, but he was not a trained historian. In his better moments, he fully recognised his limitations, but there were times when his flatterers deluded him into thinking of himself as successor to Gibbon, much in the same way that he conjured up a picture of himself as a latter-day Lorenzo in Liverpool. These day-dreams quickly vanished.

It was harsh as well as unnecessary for the Edinburgh Review critic to attribute to Roscoe 'a want of sufficient energy of thought or style',[29]

---

26   Edinburgh Review, January 1806, pp.357-358.

27   Life of W.R. Vol.1, page 334.

28   Life of W.R. Vol.1, page 333, footnote.

29   Edinburgh Review, Jan. 1806, p.358.

though perhaps he lacked the sharpness of intellect and incisive mind, which are essential attributes of a successful barrister or a master historian. Roscoe in a letter to Professor Smyth claimed rather to consider himself as 'an original historian, bringing before the public new documents, and laying before them full information, than as a writer extracting the essence of other historians and giving in a few brilliant passages a general result. On this account, I am sensible that I may at times appear prolix; but if I can give real information, I shall be well satisfied, without being considered a shining writer.'[30]

Roscoe became a great admirer of the historical writings of Guicciardini, which he asserted 'entitled their author to the indisputable precedence of all the historians of Italy, but have placed him at least on a level with those of any age or of any country.'[31] In using Guicciardini as a primary source, Roscoe also made him his model, adapting the same style and methods.

Roscoe was not 'a shining writer' and the success of his Life and Pontificate of Leo X rested not in its adequacy as a history of the revival of letters, but in its usefulness as a compendium of information in English about Pope Leo X, his predecessors and the times in which they lived.

The Edinburgh Review, after describing Roscoe's account of the origin and progress of the Reformation as 'sufficiently interesting', accused him of prejudice against Luther and partiality towards Leo X.[32] As an example of this he instanced the deliberate misdating of a letter written by Luther to Pope Leo X. According to Roscoe the famous bull of excommunication, issued against Luther by Pope Leo X in June 1520, was a justifiable response to a provocative letter sent by Luther in April of the same year. The weight of evidence suggests that the letter was written several months after the bull of excommunication was issued - that is after a succession of friendly meetings between Catholic emissaries and Luther, the object of which had been to bring about a reconciliation, which both parties had hoped for, before the papal bull came into effect. The generally accepted belief is that the later date is the correct one. Had the letter been written before the excommunication Leo X may

---

30 Life of W.R. Vol.1, page 340.

31 William Roscoe, Life of Leo X, Ch.IV, pages 164-6.

32 Edinburgh Review, January 1806, page 351.

have been justified in taking decisive action. If it had been written later in the year, when all attempts at reconciliation had failed, Luther would have appeared in a much better light and commanded more sympathy. Neither Leo X, who was liberal in outlook and disliked discord, nor Luther, desired schism. Both were driven to take action by pressures beyond their control, puppets in a conflict which had become inevitable.

Whilst Roscoe heartily approved of Luther as 'an opponent to the assumptions and gross abuses of the Roman See', he thought little of him 'as founder of a new church'.[33] He accused Luther of a fundamental inconsistency, stating that whilst Luther engaged in his opposition to the church of Rome, he asserted the right of private judgement in matters of faith with the courage and confidence of a martyr; whereas no sooner than had he freed his followers from the chains of papal domination, he forged others, in many respects more intolerable.[34] Roscoe, in defending himself against the charges of bias against Luther, declared that Luther's 'highest aim was only to establish another despotism in the place of that from which he had escaped.'[35]

In making these exaggerated pronouncements, Roscoe showed little understanding of the age in which Luther lived - an age in which religious liberty and tolerance were entirely unknown. Faced reluctantly with the novel task of founding a new church, one of Luther's first concerns was to establish an agreed basis of faith. Roscoe spoke of Luther 'laying down new doctrines', but in fact the doctrines were for the most part traditional catholic statements of faith rooted in the Bible. Roscoe, as a Unitarian, hated dogma and had little time for the traditional Christian statements of faith. In Luther's day truth was considered to be of supreme importance - worth fighting for if necessary. Luther stuck inflexibly to what he believed to be true. Roscoe in his estimate of the conduct and character of Luther refrains from mentioning his political legacy, presumably because he considered it to be outside the scope of his Life of Leo, who died within a year of Luther's excommunication. He seems to have been more concerned with Luther's religious influence than his influence in politics, despite the fact that church and state were very closely associated in those days.

---

33 William Roscoe, Life and Pontificate of Leo X (1st edition) vol.IV, pages 46-49 - quoted in Edinburgh Review, Jan. 1806.

34 Life of Leo X, Wm. Roscoe page 237 (Bohn Edition).

35 Life of W.R. Vol.1, page 338.

Roscoe's comments on the effect of the Reformation on the arts are of interest, though it is difficult to reconcile his sweeping condemnation of 'the odious and absurd institution of monastic life' with his assertion two pages earlier that certain circumstances, such as 'the silence and solemnity of the cloister', are often necessary to the complete success of the artist.[36] He continued:- 'Even the opportunity afforded the artist of a spacious repository for his productions, where they were likely to remain secure for ages, where they might be seen with every advantage of position, was a circumstance highly favourable to his success.' Roscoe failed to acknowledge the enormous debt owed to 'the absurd institution of monastic life' for preserving and creating so many treasures and valuable manuscripts through the Dark Ages and thereafter.

Roscoe was severely taken to task, in the Edinburgh Review, for his 'preposterous dissertation on the character of Lucrezia Borgia, whom our author endeavours to vindicate from the imputation of an incestuous connection with her father and two brothers.'[37] This dissertation formed the conclusion of the first volume of Roscoe's 'Life of Leo'. The reviewer asserted that the historical evidence for this relationship was reliable, quoting Gibbon's description of her conduct:

'The modern Lucrezia might have assumed with more propriety the name of Messalina, since the woman who can be guilty, who can even be accused of criminal commerce with her father and two brothers, must be abandoned to all the licentiousness of venal lust. Her vices were highly coloured by a contempt for decency. At a banquet in the apostolic palace, by the side of the Pope, she beheld, without a blush, the naked dances and lascivious postures of fifty prostitutes; she distributed the prizes to the champions of Venus, according to the number of victories which they achieved in her presence.'[38] The critic, anxious that his readers should know the full story of the papal banquet in the apostolic palace, proceeded to incorporate in his review, as a footnote, a more detailed passage in Latin from Burchard's Diary, quoted in a note from Eccard's Scriptures Mediaevi II 2134. Roscoe evidently fancied himself as a doughty defender of truth and of the unjustly maligned. His case appears to have been based entirely on the fact that Lucrezia changed her ways

---

36   Life of Leo, William Roscoe, Ch. XIX, pages 240 and 242.

37   Edinburgh Review, January 1806, page 342.

38   Gibbon's Miscellaneous Works II, 689.

and became a reformed character in the court of Ferrara, when removed
by her third marriage from the licentious manners and example of the
Vatican. Again the reviewer quoted Gibbon as having observed that
'perhaps the youth of Lucrezia Borgia had been seduced by example;
perhaps she had been satiated by pleasure; perhaps she was awed by the
authority of her new parent and husband - Hercules, Duke of Ferrara and
his son, Alphonso.'[39] The reviewer appears to have been right in suggesting
that Roscoe was the first person ever to question the historicity of Lucrezia's
incestuous relationship with her father and brothers - a relationship which
accounted for other mysterious and unexplained events at that time. Roscoe
should never have allowed himself to be diverted by his concern for
Lucrezia Borgia, nor should he have added this further irrelevance to his
already overloaded Life of Leo X. Had his friend Fuseli known in advance
of Roscoe's proposed dissertation on the character of Lucrezia, he would
certainly have nipped it in the bud!

The closing chapters of Roscoe's Life and Pontificate of Leo X are
the best. Chapter twenty-two is devoted to an account of the revival of
letters and the fine arts during Leo X's papacy and was described by the
Edinburgh Review as 'incomparably the best - a subject in which taste
and criticism are very happily displayed.'[40] This accorded well with the
opinion expressed at the time of Roscoe's death by Thomas Traill, his
friend and doctor, that owing to the pressures of business, he missed his
true vocation as a talented art historian. Many of Roscoe's friends and
admirers must have hoped for more than one out of twenty-four chapters
on this subject.[41] The reviewer did not hesitate to reproach Roscoe 'for
allowing his narrative to degenerate almost perpetually into biographical
anecdotes of learned men. The critic picked out one, which he found
particularly meaningless. It was the story of "the lewd Aretin (a poet)
who, having lampooned Tintoretto, the painter, was invited to his house
to sit for his picture; when the latter producing, instead of his pencils, a
pistol from his bosom, and desiring the affrighted poet to compose himself
till he took measure of him, aimed at him deliberately from head to foot;
adding before he released him, 'I find you are just the length of two

---

39 Edinburgh Review, Jan. 1806, p.344.

40 Edinburgh Review, Jan. 1806, p.357.

41 Thomas Traill, Memoir of William Roscoe, Edinburgh New Philosophical Journal,

pistols and a half.'[42] On the other hand the critic admitted that Roscoe's observations upon Machiavelli, Guicciardini, Paolo Giovio and many other distinguished writers, 'will be read with pleasure.'[43] Roscoe had an eye for the amusing story, however irrelevant.

The last chapter is almost completely free from digression. In it Roscoe gave a very judicious account of Leo X's character and achievements, based as always on a wide range of well documented sources. Roscoe recognised the wide diversity of opinion regarding the character of Leo X, arising inevitably out of his Medici family connection, his active role in politics and his conduct as head of the church. The Edinburgh Review's final comment on Roscoe's Life of Leo was that 'Roscoe's writings impress us with one uniform conviction, that he is a truly amiable man.'[44] Roscoe was naturally inclined to look always for the best and not the worst in other people. His chief fault as a biographer, if it is a fault, was to dwell only on the positive side of his subject's character and achievement.

Although Roscoe has left us a mine of information regarding Leo X and **his** times, no very clear picture emerges of the man himself. Roscoe's impression of Leo X seems to have been based on 'the exquisite picture of him by Raphael, which expresses the propensities, qualities and talents by which he was distinguished.'[45] The portrait attributed to Sebastiano del Piombo may well be more true to life. It corresponds closely with the down-to-earth description of Leo X on the day of his formal entry into the Vatican for his coronation and the more splendid ceremony of the procession to take possession of the Lateran a few days later. Roscoe's account of the latter is based on a very circumstantial account of this occasion by Giovanni Giacomo Penni, a Florentine physician who was present in Rome and witnessed these events.[46] The account records Leo's remark, 'We confirm, but do not assent', made on receipt of a gift of the

---

42 Edinburgh Review, Jan. 1806, p.357.

43 Edinburgh Review, Jan. 1806, p.356.

44 Edinburgh Review, Jan. 1806, p.356.

45 Wm. Roscoe, Life of Leo X (Bohn edition) page 377.

46 Wm. Roscoe, the Life of Leo X, see Fifth Edition, 1846, revised by his son, Thomas, page 482, note 218, (Bohn Edition), where Roscoe explains that Penni's account was printed in Rome in 1513 and is now of extreme rarity.

Law of Moses presented to him by Jewish residents in Rome.[47] It also mentions the loud acclamations of the populace hailing the new Pontiff, 'Leone, Leone, Palle, Palle', the name of the new Pope and the coat of arms of the Medici family.

Christopher Hibbert's description of these events in his book,[48] 'The Rise and Fall of the House of Medici', appears to be based on a similar, if not the same source as is Roscoe's, although Roscoe mentions the source of his information, whereas Hibbert does not. Hibbert's narrative might well owe its origin to the perceptive diagnosis of a Florentine physician, who witnessed the events. Despite his unprepossessing appearance, the crowds took to him immediately. 'God has given us the Papacy', Leo is reported to have said to his brother Guliano, 'Let us enjoy it.' Leo X was a new kind of Pope and there was much in him that appealed to Roscoe. Leo X was strongly influenced by his classical education and classical culture. Humanist and tolerant in outlook, he displayed little interest in theological niceties. Roscoe was full of admiration for his achievements in promoting education, learning and the arts in Rome, which had fallen far behind many lesser cities of Italy. There was something new and refreshing about a pope who enjoyed hunting, shooting and fishing during his leisure hours, and who not only enjoyed music, but could compose and who, like the Emperor Nero, could play an instrument himself. There was something new about a pope who, Roscoe assured his readers, 'exhibited not only in his early years, but after his elevation to the pontificate, an example of chastity and decorum, the more remarkable as it was unusual in the age in which he lived.'[49]

In the closing paragraphs of his Life of Leo, Roscoe found room to mention again two contemporaries who shared with Leo X 'the honours

---

47 Wm. Roscoe, Life of Leo X, (Bohn Edition) 1846, page 302.

48 Christopher Hibbert, Rise and Fall of the House of Medici, 1974, page 218:- 'As he (Pope Leo X) rode in the procession sitting side-saddle on a white Arab horse, it was noticed how his face, almost purple with the heat, ran with sweat despite the canopy of embroidered silk which was held over his head by eight Romans of distinguished birth. It was noticed, too, how corpulent he was, how vast his paunch, how fleshy his short neck, how fat the rolls beneath his chin, how bulging his weak eyes. Those whose duties brought them close to him were also distastefully aware of the smell that now and again was emitted from the huge bottom on the saddle. Yet there was something endearing about the pleasure he so obviously took in the pageant; ... His contentment was so transparent as to be infectious.'

49 William Roscoe, Life of Leo X (Bohn Edition) page 389.

due to the restorers of learning', one of whom was the notorious Lucrezia Borgia, who as Duchess of Ferrara, became a reformed character and the other 'the most learned monarch of his time, King Henry VIII of England. Evidently Leo X and the latter were on the best of terms. Roscoe unearthed and incorporated in his Life and Pontificate of Leo X correspondence following the fateful Battle of Flodden,[50] as well as letters exchanged when the Pope conferred upon the King the title, 'Defender of the Faith',[51] all documents of special interest to English readers. Leo was well able to cope with the learned and turbulent English monarch.

The Life of Leo, though it fell short of expectations as a historical work, served a useful purpose and was widely read in Europe and America, having been translated into French, German and Italian.

There must have been a considerable demand for Roscoe's Life of Leo X in England, where three editions were printed during his life-time and a further three after his death. The first edition, printed by McCreery at Liverpool, was published in 1805, comprising four volumes, each having an appendix separately paged. The work included the Dissertation on the Character of Lucrezia Borgia. Second and third editions, the latter corrected, came out in London in 1806 and 1827. Fourth and fifth editions, for the Bohn Standard Library, appeared in 1842 and 1846, the fifth edition having been revised by Roscoe's son Thomas. A further edition (two volumes) edited by W. Hazlitt came out in 1883.

The first foreign edition appeared in Paris in 1808 in four volumes - Vie et Pontificat de Leon X ... ouvrage traduit de l'Anglais par P.F. Henry, a further corrected edition appearing in 1813.[52] Henry Roscoe tells us that a German scholar, Philip Henry Conrad Henke, impressed by the merits of his father's Life of Leo, took it upon himself to prepare a

---

50 William Roscoe, Life and Pontificate of Leo X, Bohn, Vol.1, pages 320 and 321, also pages 483 and 484 and Notes 225 to 227.

At Flodden Field 'on the part of the Scots, there fell beside the King (James IV) an archbishop, two bishops, four abbots, twelve earls, seventeen barons and eight to ten thousand soldiers.'

51 Pallavic, Council di Trento, lib ii, cap i sec. viii, p.177. Pope Leo's proposed title 'Defender of the Faith' did not meet with universal approval. Among other titles for the sovereign of England suggested by the cardinals were - the Apostolic, the Orthodox, the Faithful or the Angelic!

52 Life of Wm. Roscoe by his son Henry, Vol. 1, page 348.

German translation between 1806 and 1808, enriching Roscoe's work with a preface, notes and dissertations. The first edition was printed and published in Leipzig in 1808, a second edition following ten years later in Vienna. Finally much to the delight of Roscoé a translation of his Life of Leo X appeared in Italy in 1816-17. The translator was Count Luigi Bossi, who like his German counterpart, added a variety of notes and documents illustrating Roscoe's original text. The work comprised twelve volumes and contained numerous plates of portraits and medals. Despite the fact that this work was denounced by Pope Leo Xll and consigned to the Index Expurgatorius, two thousand eight hundred copies were circulated and presumably sold in Italy.[53]

Roscoe on receipt of the earlier volumes of this Italian edition, wrote a letter to Count Bossi - 'For the favourable manner in which you have spoken of my work, and for the attention you have paid in giving a faithful version of it, I feel myself much indebted ... The disadvantages incurred by your having commenced your work from a French translation is a subject of much regret, as some of the passages omitted are essential to the course of the narrative, or consist of those reflections which naturally result from it. The omission of those passages by the French translator would be unpardonable, were there not some excuse from the wretched state of subjugation to which the press has been reduced in France by the jealousy of her rulers. You have, however, done all that is within your power to repair this defect; and in case your work should be reprinted you will, I doubt not, take care that these passages are properly restored, so that the work may be, as you express it, 'genuina ed intiera in tutte le sue parti.'[54]

---

53   Life of W.R. Vol.1, page 345.

54   Life of W.R. Vol.1, pages 346-7.

Chapter Four

Roscoe's Poetical and Other Works

In the eighteenth and nineteenth centuries a plentiful supply of ink was kept in every middle-class household. Letters had to be written every week to sons and daughters away from home. Diaries were kept conscientiously and often members of the family gave expression to their feelings in verse. Even today in the Netherlands on the Eve of the Feast of St. Nicholas (December 5th), father, mother and children are expected to write poems, place them in envelopes, and present them to other members of the family. Roscoe, himself a great lover of poetry, but not a great poet, felt a compulsion to commemorate significant events and to honour special people, to record experiences of his own and to respond to the beauty of the world around him in rhythmic verse rather than in prose.

Roscoe wrote a large number of poems in his life-time, some of which still survive in manuscript and many were printed, illustrated occasionally with a drawing of his own. The first collection of Roscoe's poems under the title the Poetical Works of William Roscoe was published in 1853 to commemorate the centenary of his birth. A further selection was compiled by George Chandler, City Librarian of Liverpool, and forms Part II of his 'William Roscoe of Liverpool' published in 1953 for the bicentenary. Sir Alfred Shennan, chairman of the Finance and General Purposes Committee of the Liverpool City Council concluded his introduction to this latter volume thus:- 'The Roscoe poems are not offered as the work of a poet even moderately great, though they are the product of a great man. They remarkably exemplify the muse, domestic and celebratory, of a cultured eighteenth century English gentleman of a Whiggish way of thought. And they help to illustrate that century's combination of classical tradition and the awakening interest in human rights and emancipation.'[1]

Roscoe's gifts as a versatile writer of poetry may well have been underestimated. In 1898 Dr Mandell Creighton, Bishop of London, was

---

1   William Roscoe of Liverpool, George Chandler, 1953 Introduction by Sir Alfred Shennan, page xxxvi.

the guest speaker at a gathering in St. George's Hall on the occasion of the Centenary of the Liverpool Athenaeum, of which Roscoe was a founder member.[2] Dr Creighton took the opportunity to pay homage to Roscoe's memory. After speaking of Roscoe's 'keen and discriminating appreciation of Robert Burns', he said 'Roscoe's admiration of Scotia's Bard is all the more remarkable, when it is remembered that the Poet's fame was not then at its zenith'. He proceeded to describe Roscoe's 'Monody on the Death of Burns as still unsurpassed as a poetic tribute to a great poet', and quoted the first stanzas as a specimen:

> 'Rear high thy bleak majestic hills,
> Thy sheltered valleys proudly spread,
> And, Scotia, pour thy thousand rills,
> And wave thy heaths and blossoms red.

> But ah! what poet now shall tread
> Thy airy heights, thy woodland reign,
> Since he the sweetest bard is dead
> That ever breathed the soothing strain'.[3]

Roscoe's earliest poem was an ode written specially to mark the inauguration in 1773 of the 'Society for the Encouragement of the Arts of Painting and Design', of which he was a founder member. It contains a comparison between music and painting, a theme to which he constantly

---

2   Liverpool Daily Post, December 20th, 1898. Dr Creighton, formerly Professor of Ecclesiastical History at Cambridge wrote a 'History of the Papacy during the Reformation', 1882, 'The Tudors and the Reformation' 1876, 'The Age of Elizabeth' 1876 and several biographies.

3   George Chandler, William Roscoe of Liverpool, Editorial Note page 324. Chandler in his selection of poems by Roscoe, which forms part of his volume for the Roscoe bi-centenary in 1953, does not include the 'Monody on the Death of Burns' because no reference to this poem is made in the Roscoe Papers and Manuscripts in the Picton Library in Liverpool and on what he describes as 'internal evidence'. Chandler was mistaken, because Roscoe's friend and collaborator, Dr Currie, stated categorically, in a letter to Mr Syme, a friend of Burns, 'I have received two monodies on Burns, one by Roscoe, another by Rushton. They have both great merit, especially the first' - See The Life of Dr Currie, Vol.1 page 268 and the Life of Wm. Roscoe, by his son Henry, Vol.1, page 235. The Monody on the Death of Burns is included in the 1853.

returned in later life. The poem contains these lines:-[4]

When just degrees of shade and light
Contend in sweetest harmony,
Then bursts upon the raptur'd sight
The silent MUSIC of the eye.
Bold, as the Base's deeper sound,
We trace the well imagin'd ground;
Next in the varying scenes behind,
The sweet melodious Tenor find;
And as the softening notes decay,
The distant prospect fades away:
Their aid if mingling colours give,
To bid the mimic landscape live;
The visual concert breaks upon the eyes,
With every different charm which Music's hand supplies.

In the same poem, Roscoe makes a comparison between the great masters of poetry and painting, displaying his taste for the arts as well as literature.

Majestic, nervous, bold, and strong,
Let ANGELO with MILTON vie;
Oppos'd to WALLER's amorous song,
His art let wanton TITIAN try;
Let great ROMANO'S free design,
Contend with DRYDEN's pompous line;
And chaste CORREGGIO'S graceful air,
With POPE'S unblemish'd page compare;
LORAINE may rival THOMSON'S name;
And HOGARTH's equal BUTLER'S fame:

Edition of Roscoe's Poems.

4   Ditto, pages 327-8.

For still where-e'er th'aspiring Muse

Her wide, unbounded flight pursues,

Her Sister soars on kindred wings sublime,

And gives her favourite names to grace the rolls of time.

Roscoe's first major poem was Mount Pleasant, also written before he attained the age of twenty, in which he celebrated the growing importance of his native town, deplored the evils of the slave trade and the commercial thirst for gain when too much indulged:

"Ah! why, ye sons of wealth, with ceaseless toil,

Add gold to gold, and swell the shining pile?

Your general course to happiness ye bend:

Why, then, to gain the means, neglect the end?"[5]

Roscoe's next major poem (1787) 'The Wrongs of Africa' was welcomed by the Society for the Abolition of the Slave Trade in London as a useful contribution to its propaganda campaign.[6] Roscoe's original intention was to write a poem consisting of three parts - the first describing the character of the slave trade along the coast of West Africa - the second the crossing of the Atlantic Ocean - and the third the West Indian plantations. The last part was never written. Roscoe denounces the slave traders with great fervour:

'Whilst he, the white deceiver, who had sown

The seeds of discord, saw with horrid joy

The harvest ripen to his utmost wish;

And reap'd the spoils of treachery, guilt and blood.'[7]

Roscoe was fully aware that many of his clients, friends and neighbours were to be numbered among the 'white deceivers'. A contemporary Liverpool journalist and critic, who wrote under the pseudonym of Sypher, commenting upon anti-slavery propaganda of the time, remarked 'British anti-slavery literature was so firmly set in a neo-classical form that even the most knowledgeable observers of the slave trade adopted its conventions when they lapsed into verse. The hero was almost

---

5   Liverpool Abolitionists, F.E.Sanderson Appendix p.228.

6   Liverpool Abolitionists, F.E.Sanderson Appendix p.228.

7   Roscoe of Liverpool, George Chandler, page 352.

inevitably an African of noble birth, idealised out of all semblance of reality, a pseudo-African in a pseudo-Africa, yearning for freedom, speaking the traditional language of rebellion against oppression and dying in circumstances of high drama'.[8] Roscoe's poem, the wrongs of Africa is heady stuff and one wonders what effect it had, if any, on the campaign for abolition.

Poems on Freedom

Henry Roscoe tells us that the first time his father appears to have taken any public part in politics was in 1788, the centenary of the peaceful English Revolution. A number of gentlemen of Liverpool gathered to celebrate the occasion, one of whom was Roscoe who recited a commemorative poem, composed by himself, entitled 'A Secular Song of the Revolution', in which he proudly praised the English liberties secured in 1688, each stanza ending with the rousing refrain:

'Then grasp the deep bowl, the full chorus prolong,

To William and Freedom be sacred the song.'[9]

Henry also tells us that his father's native disposition displayed itself in an attachment to the principles of freedom and in an opposition to injustice and oppression under every form.[10] It is not surprising, therefore, that Roscoe and others, like Wordsworth, who shared his views welcomed the outbreak of the French Revolution with keen interest and a degree of sympathy, imagining it to be a French movement similar to the peaceful Revolution in England. Roscoe hastened to celebrate the event by publishing in 1789 an 'Ode to the People of France', in imitation of a Canzone of Petrarch, which was much admired by Charles Fox, the Whig Leader.[11] This poem is an invocation to 'Liberty' personified, which reflects Roscoe's recognition of the value of the gift of freedom:

---

8   Liverpool Abolitionists, F.E. Sanderson Note 70 Transactions of the History Society of Lancashire and Cheshire.

9   Life of W.R. Vol1 pages 103-4.

10 Life of W. R. Vol.1 pages 1 03-4.

11 Life of W.R. Vol.1, page 106.

'Freedom! blest gift, whom none condemn who know;

Dear is thy presence to this world below!

Life vigorous grows where'er thy steps have trod,

And man walks forth the semblance of a God;

If thou be absent, life no joy affords,

Despised its titled pomps, its useless hoards;

But in thy presence every cottage charms,

And Peace reposes in thy sheltering arms.'

So great was the interest of Roscoe and his Liverpool friends in the progress of the French Revolution that a meeting was held on July 14, 1790 to celebrate the Fall of the Bastille.[12] On this occasion Roscoe introduced another popular song of his own beginning with the words:

'Unfold Father Time! thy long records unfold

Of noble achievements accomplished of old...'

The first stanza ends with the couplet:

"While France rises up, and confirms the decree

That tears off her chains, and millions be free."

The second and third verses end again with a rousing chorus for all to join in:

"Seize then the glad moment, and hail the decree

That bids millions rejoice, and a nation be free!"[13]

A year later Roscoe wrote yet another revolutionary song, the best known of them all, which came to be known as 'the Day-star of Liberty', and which was intended for use on the second anniversary of the French Revolution in 1791. However, owing to riots in Birmingham, the celebrations in Liverpool and elsewhere were abandoned.[14] This was the song Robert Burns greatly admired and copied in his own hand. The

---

12 Life of W.R. Vol.1, page 106.

13 Life of W.R. Vol.1, pages 105 and 108.

14 Life of W.R. Vol.1, pages 105 and 108.

poem was published anonymously and it was not generally known that Roscoe was the author until as late as 1812. The poem begins with the lines:

> O'er the vine-cover'd hills and gay regions of France,
>
> See the day-star of Liberty rise.

Those of Roscoe's friends who studied the third verse of the 'Day-star of Liberty' may well have guessed the name of the author:

> Let Burke like a bat from its splendour retire,
>
> A splendour too strong for his eyes;
>
> Let pedants and fools his effusions admire,
>
> Entrapt in his cobwebs like flies.
>
> Shall insolent Sophistry hope to prevail
>
> Where reason opposes her weight,
>
> When the welfare of millions is hung in the scale,
>
> And the balance yet trembles with fate?

It was in the previous year that Burke published his 'Reflections on the Revolution in France' (1790), a book described by Chandler as 'a symbol for the English horror of the French revolutionary violence'.[15] Roscoe never forgave Burke for deserting the Whigs and for forsaking the reforming movement in England of which he had been a strong supporter before the French Revolution.

'The Day-star of Liberty' was Roscoe's last revolutionary poem. Henry Roscoe tells us that 'Those who like his father, had witnessed with delight the birth of freedom in France, and watched anxiously over its cradle, and who had looked for peace, and happiness, and improvement, as the great results of the revolution, beheld with grief and dismay the alarming vicissitudes of its progress. The last hope of the friends of France seemed to expire on the scaffold of the Brissotines.'[16]

---

15 Chandler, Wm. Roscoe of Liverpool page 70.

16 Life of W.R. Vol.1, page 110.

The Brissotines, better known as the Girondins, were the Deputies of France who formed the leadership of the newly elected National Assembly, and who consisted of 'a body of young and eloquent men of the middle class ... drawn from the south-western area of France called the Gironde ... they possessed and were able to communicate to others, a glowing enthusiasm for the republican idea, and a missionary impulse to spread it through Europe. Vergniaud and Isnard were the orators, Brissot the diplomatic adviser, the wife of Roland the Egeria of the party. The dazzling dreams, the sentimental enthusiasm, and the tragic end of the Girondins have secured them many friends.' H.A.L. Fisher, History of Europe, page 808.

The greater part of Roscoe's early poems, including his numerous love songs and lyrics written during the long years of his engagement, and referred to in the first chapter, are written in a serious vein. As he matured he began to take others and himself less seriously. In 1791 he wrote and published a splendid ballad entitled 'The Life, Death and Wonderful Achievements of Edmund Burke'.[17] Roscoe was a great admirer of Fox, who unlike Burke, courageously held fast to his political ideals and refused to allow his concern for reform in England to be affected by events in France. The poem was accompanied by a frontispiece consisting of a drawing of his own, representing Burke armed like a knight, attacking Mr Fox in the House of Commons.

> Full tilt he ran at all he met,
> > And round he dealt his knocks,
> Till with a backward stroke at last
> > He hit poor CHARLEY FOX.
>
> Now CHARLEY was of all his friends,
> > The warmest friend he had;
> So when he felt this graceless blow,
> > He deem'd the man was mad.
>
> With grief his generous bosom rose,
> > A grief too great to hide;
> And as the stroke was somewhat hard,
> > He sat him down and cry'd.
>
> But not a whit did EDMUND feel,
> > For at his friend he flew,
> Resolved before the neighbours round
> > To beat him black and blue.

---

17 George Chandler, William Roscoe of Liverpool. Part 2. Pages 388-9.

Then CHARLES indignant started up
　　The meagre form he took,
And with a giant's awful grasp
　　His rusty armour shook.

O have ye seen a mastiff strong
　　A shivering lap-dog tear?
- Then may ye judge how EDMUND did
　　When claw'd by CHARLES appear.

　Roscoe numbered among his friends and acquaintances Mary Wollstonecraft, a staunch pioneer of the women's liberation movement, author of a 'Vindication of the Rights of Women', published in 1792. The poem goes on to tell the story of how Burke, after having been clawed by Charley Fox in the House of Commons, escaped ignominiously and roamed the countryside in search of sympathy. Suddenly he was taken by surprise by Wollstonecraft, who attacked him wielding a cudgel made of oak. His coat of rusty steel offered him scant protection:

And wild he roam'd the country round
　　And angry scours the streets,
And tweaks the nose, or kicks the breech
　　Of ev'ry Whig he meets.

The neighbours first were all surpriz'd
　　Then sorry as he past
Then laughed his antic freaks to see,
　　But angry grew at last.

An lo! an Amazon steps out,
　　One WOLLSTONECRAFT her name,
Resolved to stop his mad career,
　　Whatever chance became.

An oaken fapling in her hand,
  Full on the foe she fell,
Nor could his coat of rusty steel,
  Her vig'rous strokes repel.

When strange to see, her conq'ring staff,
  Returning leaves o'erspread,
Of which a verdant wreath was wove,
  And bound around her head.[18]

Mary Wollstonecraft married William Godwin, a dissenting minister turned atheist philosopher, holding anarchic views. She died in 1797 at the birth of her daughter Mary, who was to marry the poet, Shelley. At her death Roscoe wrote a little poem:

Hard was thy fate in all the scenes of life
  As daughter, sister, parent, friend and wife,
But harder still in death thy fate we own,
  Mourn'd by thy Godwin - with a heart of stone.[19]

Roscoe was a keen observer of nature, and a close study of insect life always intrigued him. Anyone who has carefully watched a spider attempting to capture a bee or a wasp in its web, cannot fail to appreciate 'The True Story of the Spider and the Bee', an exciting and artless story of a daily occurrence in summer-time:

With viscous thread and finger fine,
  The spider spun his filmy line;
Th'extremes with stronger cordage tied,
  And wrought the web from side to side.

---

18 George Chandler, William Roscoe of Liverpool, Part 2, Pages 389, 390.

19 Roscoe Papers 3958 A (on Mary Wollstonecraft).

**Mary Wollstonecraft, 1759-97,
to whom Roscoe referred in his poem on Burke.**
From the painting in the Roscoe Collection, Walker Art Gallery, Liverpool
"An lo! an Amazon stept out
one Wolstonecraft her name."

Beneath the casement's pendant roof
    He hung aloft the shadowy woof;
There in the midst compress'd he lies,
    And patient waits th'expected prize.

When lo! on sounding pinion strong,
    A bee incautious rush'd along;
Nor of the gauzy net aware,
    Till all entangled in the snare.

Enrag'd, he plies his sounding wings,
    His far-resounding war-song sings;
Tears all that would his course control,
    And threatens ruin to the whole.

With dread, with gladness, with surprise,
    The spider saw his dangerous prize;
Then rush'd relentless on his foe,
    Intent to give the deadly blow.

But as the spider came in view,
    The bee his poison'd dagger drew;
Back at the sight the spider ran,
    And cautiously his work began.

With lengthen'd arms the snares he plied,
    He turn'd the bee from side to side;
His legs he tied, his wings he bound
    And whirled him round and round and round.

And then, with cautious steps and slow,
He came to give the fatal blow;
When frightened at the trenchant blade,
The bee one desperate effort made.

The fabric breaks, the cords give way,
His wings resume their wonted play;
Far off on gladsome plume he flies,
And drags the spider through the skies.

Thus once Lunardi sailed along,
The wonder of the gazing throng;
Uncertain where his course to bend,
And where his lengthen'd flight might end.[20]

Perhaps the most popular of all Roscoe's poems were those written for his family, which first appeared in print in 1806, The Butterfly's Ball and The Grasshopper's Feast.[21] Within two months John Harris, owner of the Juvenile Library at the corner of St. Paul's Churchyard in London, published these poems in paper-back, illustrated with drawings by William Mulready and sold for a shilling plain or one and sixpence coloured - a high price in those days.[22] In these imaginative poems Roscoe personified creatures great and small, and unlike Aesop's Fables the poems are totally lacking in moral content. They are written for the amusement of the young in heart and to encourage children to appreciate the world of nature. There is no place in these poems for fairies, magic and witches. Roscoe found himself faced with competition from Mrs Dorset, who imitating his work, came forward with "The Peacock's 'At Home'" in September 1807, followed by 'The Elephant's Ball', 'The

---

20 Poems for Youth by a Family Circle, 1820, p.9 also George Chandler, Roscoe of Liverpool, p.426. The bee's flight reminded Roscoe of Leonardo da Vinci's experiment with wings.

21 The Gentleman's Magazine, November 1806.

22 The Times, September 26, 1973 - Review of New Edition under the head 'The Animal Kingdom of the Kindly Mr Roscoe'.

Lion's Masquerade' and 'The Lobster's Voyage to the Brazils', were published by the enterprising Mr Harris, 40,000 copies of each being sold in the first year of publication. Roscoe published a further poem - 'The Butterfly's Birthday' in 1809. When Roscoe put pen to paper and wrote 'The Butterfly's Ball', he would never have guessed that he was to become a pioneer in this literary field, followed by Beatrix Potter, Kenneth Grahame, Alison Uttley and a host of others. Hartley Coleridge, writing in 1836, tells us that these ballads, though published as a child's book, have the true spirit of faery poesy and remind one of the best things of Herrick.

Roscoe's poem entitled 'The Squirrel' always reminds me of the stuffed red squirrel, possibly a family heirloom, given to my brothers and me, when small children, by our great-aunt Beatrice, the daughter of Laura Roscoe (Mrs James Thornely), who was a grand-daughter of William Roscoe. In the Roscoe tradition 'Squirrel' was a real person and very much one of the family. As far as I can remember, Squirrel had a peculiar way of speaking and was very much of a character, having decided opinions of his own. In Roscoe's day and for many years after, animal lovers had no compunction about stuffing birds and beasts or sticking pins through butterflies. Roscoe's 'The Squirrel' is one of 'the Poems for Youth by a Family Circle', 1820.

> I love to see at early morn
>> The Squirrel sport before my door;
>> There crack his nuts and hide his shells,
>> Or leap away for more.

> I love to hear the black birds note
>> Loud swelling from th'ivied spray,
>> And sweet to me at dewy dawn
>> The Red breasts wild untutor'd lay.

> For sure when Nature's free born train
>> Approach with song and gambol near,
>> Some secret impulse bids them feel
>> The footsteps of a friend are near.[23]

---

23 Roscoe Papers 3869 -
   and George Chandler - Wm. Roscoe of Liverpool, page 196.

Roscoe, with the help of some friends, prepared for publication in 1818 a new edition of a hymn-book for use by the congregation of the Renshaw Street Unitarian Chapel, of which he was a life-long member. The new book contained seven hymns composed by himself, some of which are very similar in style and content to other hymns of the period. His anthem "Holy, Holy, Holy, Lord God Almighty" bears a close resemblance to Bishop Heber's Trinity Sunday hymn, beginning with exactly the same words and written at the same time. Heber's hymn is incomparably better, not because it is Trinitarian, but because it is flawless! As well as writing a pleasing paraphrase of the Lord's Prayer in verse, Roscoe produced a concise version of Our Lord's Summary of the Law in two neat stanzas, which could prove useful to anyone planning a back-to-basics campaign:

> What is the first and great command?
>
> To love thy God above:
>
> And what the second? As thyself
>
> Thy neighbour thou shalt love.

> Who is my neighbour? He who wants
>
> The help which thou canst give:
>
> And both the law and prophets say
>
> This do and thou shalt live.[24]

Roscoe may not have been a great poet. He certainly did not lack versatility and with a little expert help and guidance, he might well have become a workmanlike Poet Laureate, ready to write for every imaginable occasion. Much of his work may seem démodé nowadays, but some of his more unaffected poems can still give pleasure.

George Chandler, in his book published for the Roscoe bi-centenary in 1953, told us that 'whatever Roscoe did he did with distinction'. It is curious that he should have made this remark in a short paragraph in which he dismissed the longest and most elaborate of Roscoe's publications in nine words:- 'his edition of Pope led to a long controversy'.[25] Roscoe's edition of 'The Works of Alexander Pope Esq.'

---

24 George Chandler - Wm. Roscoe of Liverpool, page 422.
25 George Chandler, William Roscoe of Liverpool, page 132.

published in 1824, included a life of Pope, five hundred and eighty five pages in all, and nine other volumes containing selected poems complete with commentary and notes.

When Roscoe in 1821 was approached by some London booksellers requesting him to prepare a new edition of the works of Pope, he agreed without hesitation. From his earliest days he had been an admirer of Pope, one of whose poems he had included in his 'Select Poems extracted from Several Authors' in 1770 at the age of seventeen. Roscoe felt an affinity with Pope because he came from a similar background, having had no formal education and having had rather similar experiences in his youth. Roscoe believed that the principal object of the new edition was the need for a fuller and more accurate life of the poet than had yet appeared. The second reason was that previous editors, notably Johnson and the Revd. W. Bowles 'had with a prejudice which appears in every page depreciated the genius and assailed the moral character of the poet.'[26] The motives which prompted Roscoe to spring to the defence of Pope were uncannily similar to those which made him rally to the defence of Lorenzo the Magnificent a quarter of a century earlier. Previous editions of Pope aroused considerable controversy in which Lord Byron, Thomas Campbell, the Quarterly Review and others were active participants. While the disputants were contending for victory, Roscoe ventured into the field - a veritable minefield - with vigour if not always with discretion. Much of the heated argument was not about the merits of Pope's poetry, but about his moral character.

The Quarterly review critic gave a favourable welcome to Roscoe's edition of Pope's works, remarking that 'Mr Roscoe's selection from his predecessors is also copious and judicious - so copious that as far as regards Mr Bowles' book, which may be considered as a rival publication in the market, we know not how these writers adjust their claim, for he has without ceremony taken much of what is valuable in Mr Bowles' book to add to the value of his own. His original criticism is not much, but is enlightened and liberal and the candour with which that and the life are written is quite refreshing after the blighting perversity of the preceding editors, whose misrepresentations and calumnies he had industriously examined and patiently refuted. Great industry is exhibited in the superior arrangement of his materials. He has given an index only to the volume containing his life. We wish he had imitated Mr Bowles in

---

26   Life of W.R. Vol 2, p 334-5

giving a general index.'[27] The most significant alteration Roscoe made in his edition was the omission of certain poems which he believed did the poet little credit. Roscoe considered it to be the chief duty of an editor to execute an office which the author can do longer do for himself.[28] This Roscoe asserted was the principle upon which Pope acted in regard to the poet, John Gay, for whom he was an executor.[29] The Quarterly Review critic supporting Roscoe's opinion on this matter made this pronouncement:- 'when editors gratify their own pruriency or that of those who buy their books, by reviving pieces written in the levity of youth or exuberance of wit, but suppressed in maturer age and by improved judgement: or the productions of an hour of inconsiderate gaiety, never meant for indiscriminate perusal, let the future evil and disgrace be on their hands. It was Pope's wish, in purgation of his works, to defecate as much as possible the source, and purify the stream for posterity, but Mr Bowles, in particular has industriously sought out secret depositories of the dregs and thrown them again into the stream. Mr Roscoe's edition is honourably distinguished by a very different spirit.'[30] The Rev. W.L. Bowles is further accused of taking 'a festive delight in vilification'.

One of the controversial matters, which Roscoe dealt with in his Life of Pope, was the assertion by Warton, an earlier editor of Pope's works, to the effect that Pope 'had acknowledged himself an unbeliever in Christianity'.[31] Roscoe was able on the basis of three letters written by Pope to Samuel Richardson and preserved by Mr J.L. Anderton, to prove the allegations to be totally untrue.[32] Roscoe informed his readers 'that Pope himself told us that he was neither Papist nor Protestant, but something between the two:- Like good Erasmus, in an honest mean.'[33] Roscoe continued 'He was too acquainted with the genuine doctrines of Christianity to suppose that all merit consisted in the profession of a

---

27 Quarterly Review, October, 1825 pages 276 and 277.

28 Life of W.R. Vol. 2, page 340.

29 Life of Pope by Wm. Roscoe p.368 - Pope is quoted as having said "Our poor friend's papers are in my hands; and for as much as is so, I will take care to suppress things unworthy of him".

30 Quarterly Review, October 1825 p.273 et seq.

31 Wm. Roscoe, Life of Pope, p.388.

32 Wm. Roscoe, Life of Pope, p.388.

33 Wm. Roscoe, Life of Pope, page 572.

particular creed: and he held in abhorrence the uncharitable doctrine, by whatever sect advanced, which pretends to limit within its own pale, the universal goodness of God'. Roscoe asserted that these sentiments were strongly expressed by Pope at different periods of his life. The sentiments were fully shared by Roscoe himself.

Roscoe was on less sure ground when he defended Pope's translation of Homer's Iliad. Previous editors had criticised this poem on the ground that it was a grossly inaccurate translation, written by a poet whose knowledge of ancient Greek was very limited. The Quarterly Review critic suggested that 'Poetic pleasure, not archaeological information was the prime object of Pope'.[34] He also raised the question whether Homer could have given so much pleasure to the English reader in any other form. Pope's picture of Homeric Greece was far removed from the reality at times, as indeed was Roscoe's picture of Florence in the days of Lorenzo.

Roscoe rarely missed an opportunity of telling a good story in his biographical works. He cast a new light on Pope's eccentricity when he told the story of how, on the death of the poet's mother in 1733 at the age of ninety-one, Pope sent an urgent message to Jonathan Richardson, an artist of some renown, inviting him to come and paint a portrait of his deceased mother.[35] Speaking of the proposed portrait, he wrote in his letter 'It would afford the finest image of a saint expired, that ever painting drew, and it would be the greatest obligation which even that obliging art could ever bestow upon a friend. I shall hope to see you this evening as late as you will, or tomorrow morning as early as before this winter-flower is faded. I will defer her interment until tomorrow night.' Roscoe tells us that to a request made in such terms, the painter was not insensible and that a portrait was accordingly taken which has since been engraved and may still serve to give some idea of those features which were regarded by Pope with such filial affection and respect.

A few months after publication of Roscoe's edition of the works of Pope, the Prebendary W.L. Bowles, Fellow of the Royal Society of Literature, published a booklet entitled 'A Final Appeal to the Literary Public, in Reply to Certain Observations of Mr Roscoe in his Edition of the Works of Pope. This prompted a reply from Roscoe which provoked a further publication by Bowles entitled 'Lessons in Criticism to William

---

34 Quarterly Review, October, 1825, page 294.

35 Wm. Roscoe - Life of Pope, page 370.

Roscoe Esq. F.R.S., Member of the Della Crusca Society of Florence, F.R.S.L., in Answer to His Letter to the Rev. W.L. Bowles on the Character and Poetry of Pope. With further Lessons in Criticism, to a Quarterly Reviewer'. Roscoe was sorely tempted to write again. He did in fact write a draft reply, expressing regret 'if he had transgressed the bounds of civility, which he had a right to expect in return', and 'he would not, like Mr Bowles, congratulate himself on his triumph, but would leave it to the public to decide between them'. Deciding that enough was enough, he refrained from sending the letter.[36] Roscoe's blatant plagiarism, for which he appears to have made no apology, must have caused considerable provocation to his literary antagonist, Mr Bowles. Roscoe should have confined himself only to writing a Life of Pope, a task for which he was well qualified. He should not have responded to the request for a new edition of the works of Pope.

The writer of the Quarterly Review critique of Roscoe's edition of Pope's works expressed the opinion that:- 'It is therefore high, perhaps the highest in the second class, that we must rank the poetic genius of Pope'. For him the top class consisted of Shakespeare, Milton and Spenser only. He also made the platitudinous, but nevertheless true, pronouncement:- 'Much in the judgement of every individual will depend that individual's tastes and sympathies'. Roscoe derived great pleasure from the works of Pope. He may well have overrated Pope's genius; many of Pope's critics underrated him.

Roscoe's comparison of the works of Swift and Pope, which forms the final paragraph of his Life of Pope, was the last and perhaps the best of his writings on a literary subject. It was inspired by observations on the same theme by Sir Walter Scott.[37]

'When we turn to the perusal of Swift, we observe the workings of an original and vigorous mind, expending itself in objects of a temporary or local nature, or in dark or sombre pictures of the different relations of human life, in which we seldom sympathise, and from which we occasionally turn with disgust. Even his wit and his humour are often of so cynical a kind as to prevent our indulging ourselves in them, without something like self-reproach at the nature of our own feelings; whilst the writings of Pope, on the other hand, contain an inexhaustible fund of

---

36 Life of W.R. Vol.2 pages 344-5.

37 Wm. Roscoe, Life of Pope, first volume of his edition of 'the Works of Alexander Pope'.

the most magnanimous and generous sentiments, the love of virtue, the delights of friendship, the value of independence, the indispensable duty of submission to the Divine will, the blessings derived from human society, and various other topics of the highest importance to our welfare, expressed in language which, whilst it convinces the judgement, touches the heart, and whilst it never tires on repetition, is calculated, more perhaps than that of any other author, to impress similar ideas and sentiments on the minds of millions yet to come'.

Roscoe took immense pride in his last published work, described by Chandler as 'the most distinguished labour of his old age', on Monandrian Plants.[38] No expense was spared in the production and printing of this labour of love, which occupied much of his time between 1824 and 1828, when the book was issued in parts. It consists of a large folio volume containing illustrations, some by the author's hand.

Roscoe through his interest in botany became friendly and corresponded with some of Britain's leading botanists, among whom were Sir James E. Smith and Sir William Jackson Hooker. After the death of Linnaeus, the great Swedish naturalist and founder of modern botany, in 1788, Sir James Smith, hearing that Linnaeus' precious papers were being put up for sale by his heirs, rushed over to Sweden and despite last-minute intercession by the King, bought the priceless collection for £1,000 and took it back to England.[39] Another associate of Roscoe, Sir William Jackson Hooker of Glasgow, employed Thomas Drummond as a plant hunter, in the early nineteenth century in the United States of America. Drummond was able to ship to his boss seven hundred species of plants, a hundred and fifty birds and a collection of mosses which 'sent Hooker into a botanical ecstasy'.[40] Just as a flower from America was called after Drummond, the familiar Phlox Drummondi, a flower from Nepal was named Roscoea. Roscoe was well placed in Liverpool to obtain exotic plants from far off lands for himself or for the Liverpool Botanic Garden with the help of merchant shipping friends.

---

38   George Chandler, William Roscoe of Liverpool, page 132.

39   Joseph Kastner, A World of Naturalists, 1978, page 189.

40   Joseph Kastner, A World of Naturalists, 1978, page 189.

William Roscoe, F.I.S.   *Sir James E. Smith, F.R.S., P.L.S.*

Dr. Nathaniel Wallich, F.R.S.   *Sir William J. Hooker, F.R.S.*

William Roscoe and his botanical associates

H. Stansfield in introducing an essay on William Roscoe, Botanist in the Liverpool Bulletin in 1955 wrote:

'In the mountains, at 9000 feet, in North Western Himalaya and Nepal, grow plants of a small distinguished group, the Roscoeas. They have raised their flowers to the eternal heights for countless ages; they will repeat their life-rhythms for - who knows! - long beyond the span of humans on Earth. The memorials of men to their illustrious kin, created in statuary or paintings will crumble and fade; The Roscoeas will persist, and each season, in freshness and brightness perpetuate the memory of a remarkable Liverpool gentleman - William Roscoe.'[41]

---

41 H. Stansfield, William Roscoe, Botanist, The Liverpool Bulletin, Volume 5 Nos 1 and 2, November 1955.

Chapter Five

Roscoe's Library

The Revd. James Aspinall, in his little book, "'Roscoe's Library' published in 1853 and intended for young readers says: 'It may be that there are incredulous persons among the younger generation who will say, 'You tell us indeed about Roscoe's Library - but where is it? Is it a tradition, a legend, a myth? Or has it ever been in existence. Was it ever a substantial reality? Show it to us! Seeing is believing'".

Roscoe's Library was not a figment of the imagination; it was a substantial reality, which came into existence when, as a boy of little more than twelve years of age, he made for himself a wooden book-case with folding doors to contain a small collection of books he had already acquired, the most precious of which was 'The Matchless Orinda', a collection of poems by Mrs. Catherine Philips.[1] Over a period of nearly fifty years, he steadily added to his collection, never missing an opportunity to buy books, which interested him, if and when he could afford to do so. When at the age of forty-six he took up residence at Allerton Hall, he had already built up a sizeable library. Roscoe's choice of Allerton Hall as a home, in which to live in retirement, must have been largely determined by its suitability as a place in which to accommodate his rapidly expanding collection of books. The house was much in need of renovation. Roscoe's son, Henry, tells us that the older part of the house had become dangerous from the decay of the timbers, and that his father decided to demolish and rebuild it on a uniform plan, and that in the construction of the new building, he secured for himself 'a handsome and capacious library'.[2] The alterations, which took over two years to complete, were not finished until the autumn of 1812, when at last Roscoe was able to take possession of his new library. During the Allerton years, 1799 to 1816, Roscoe was at the height of his prosperity, and was able to finance not only the building operations, but also to add very considerably to his stock of books.[3] It

---

1   Life of W.R.Vol.1, pp.10 and 11.

2   Life of W.R. Vol.2, pp.53 and 54.

3   Roscoe Papers, 3872 B. Property tax due from William Roscoe at Allerton Hall in 1806 showed him to be a man of considerable wealth.

Roscoe's Residence, 1799 to 1816:
ALLERTON HALL
in which he secured for himself 'a handsome and capacious library'
(From Mayer Papers, Picton Reference Library, Liverpool)

was at this time that he was confined to the house for several months owing to a severe and prolonged attack of sciatica. His son, Henry, tells us - "The arrangement and cataloguing of his books ... afforded him the greatest pleasure and induced him to resume the study of biography, a pursuit which during the composition of the 'Life of Leo' had necessarily occupied some share of his attention. He entered with no little ardour into this renewed pursuit, and formed the design of illustrating the origin and progress of the art of printing, by a continued series of early printed books. The sale of some valuable collections in London favoured this design, and he became the purchaser of many rare and curious specimens of early typography."[4]

Roscoe, having completed the arrangement of his books and paintings in Allerton Hall, decided to prepare a printed catalogue for publication but was prevented by sickness and other preoccupations from carrying it into effect. The draft title page for this proposed volume gives us an outline of the contents of his collection:-[5]

"Catalogue of a Private Collection of Books, Pictures, Drawings, Medals, and Prints, illustrating the Rise, Vicissitudes, and Establishment of Literature and Art in Europe; to which are added, Collectiones Medicianae, or Pieces chiefly relating to the Family of the Medici, from MSS. and rare Books in this Collection, with numerous Portraits, Facsimiles, Engravings, and Vignettes, and occasional Remarks, biographical, historical, and critical."

Roscoe proudly prepared the following Latin inscription as a prefix to his catalogue:

HÆC MONUMENTA
ARTIUM LITERARUMQUE RENASCENTIUM
PRÆCIPUE SUB AUSPICIIS
COSMI LAURENTIIQUE
NECNON LEONIS X. PONT. MAX.
DIUTURNO STUDIO CONQUISITA
COLLEGIT
DISPOSUIT
IN DELICIIS HABUIT
ATQUE POSTERITATI COMMENDAT
GULIELMUS ROSCOE.
MDCCCXV.

---

4   Life of W.R., Vol.2, p.54, Henry Roscoe does not supply details, prices, etc. of purchases made.

5   Life of W.R., Vol.2, page 56, which contains the list of contents and the inscription which was not published in the catalogue.

Within two years Roscoe found himself occupied with the same task in very different circumstances - as he sadly prepared a catalogue for the sale by auction of all his treasures, forced upon him by his bankruptcy in 1816. The collapse of Roscoe's bank necessitated not only the realisation of the assets of the bank itself, but also the disposal of the private property of the partners, including Allerton Hall, Roscoe's library and his art collections. His library was not a haphazard assortment of books acquired over a period of fifty years. It had been carefully built up with the purpose of illustrating the revival of learning (the Renaissance), which Roscoe considered 'interesting in itself and likely to prove useful to others, whose studies were directed to the literary history of the period.'[6] The Rev. William Shepherd wrote to Roscoe early in 1816, expressing sympathy, stating 'that the idea of the dispersion of your library was a subject of painful contemplation to many of your friends'.[7] The sale of Roscoe's library became necessary, but its dispersal was regrettable. The Rev. James Aspinall, writing twenty-two years after Roscoe's death said 'Liverpool allowed Roscoe's Library to be consigned to the ruthless hammer of the auctioneer. We are not going to say what 'Deus ex machina' should have stepped in and prevented such an act of Vandalism. Various judgements have been pronounced upon it. Some think the Corporation should have purchased this magnificent collection of books on behalf of the public. Some affirm that the public should have stimulated the Corporation to do so. Others allege that the public should have averted the shame by a subscription.

But we give no opinions. We make no accusations. We attempt no apportionment of blame. We only record that the thing was done. The sacrilege was perpetrated.'[8] Roscoe's paintings fared better than his books. In 1819 thirty seven paintings were hung in the Liverpool Royal Institution with the following explanation:

> 'A few individuals, conceiving that, as the following PICTURES form a series from the commencement of the Art to the close of the fifteenth century, their value would be enhanced by their being

---

6   Life of W.R., Vol.2, p.56.

7   Life of W.R., Vol.2, p.120.

8   'Roscoe's Library' by James Aspinall, 1853 page 22.

The 'sacrilege' reminded Aspinall of the action of the Caliph Omar, who, at the capture of Alexandria, condemned its splendid library, the accumulation of ages, to the flames.

perceived together, having united in purchasing and presenting them to the Liverpool Royal Institution: in the hope that, by preventing the dispersion of a collection interesting to the history, and exemplifying the progress of Design, they may contribute to the advancement of the FINE ARTS in the Town of Liverpool.'

Thus a considerable number of Roscoe's paintings were saved from dispersion. In 1893 most of the paintings, owned by the Liverpool Royal Institution, were placed on long term loan for display in the Walker Art Gallery. After the re-opening following the Second World War, these paintings were presented to the Walker Art Gallery as a permanent gift. Roscoe's outstanding group of early Italian and North European paintings, collected between 1804 and 1816, form the heart of the gallery. Among the aims of the Liverpool Royal Institution defined in 1814, were the 'collection of books, specimens of art, natural history etc.' It was unfortunate that Roscoe's most precious books, as well as his paintings, all illustrating or relating to the revival of learning, the Renaissance period, were not preserved together for the public benefit.

Roscoe insisted on preparing catalogues for the sale of his books, manuscripts, drawings and paintings. The preface to the third catalogue ends with this statement: 'Hopes had been indulged by the present possessor that the works of Literature and Art included in this, and the two preceding Catalogues, might have formed the basis of a more extensive collection, and have been rendered subservient to some object of public utility; but the circumstances of the times are not favourable to his views, and they are now offered to the public, in detail, and without reserve. The Catalogues may serve, however to give an idea of the entire collection, when the works that compose it are again dispersed.'[9]

Roscoe having completed the catalogue for the sale of his books, sent it to the printer, Mr McCreery, with precise instructions, explaining, 'As it will contain many curious books, I do not want it to be a common sale catalogue', adding ruefully, 'One would not, sure, be ugly when one's dead'.[10] The books in the catalogue comprised his entire library, with the exception of books, which had been presented to him by his friends. 'These', he told the printer emphatically, 'I shall not part with until my grasp is relaxed by death or the law'.[11] The sale of his books,

---

9 Catalogue of Drawings and Pictures, the Property of Wm. Roscoe 1816, Advertisement, Liverpool..

10 Life of W.R., Vol.2, p.115.

11 Life of W.R. Vol.2 p.119.

which commenced on August 19th 1816, lasted fourteen days. One thousand seven hundred and eighty seven works, many of them consisting of several volumes, were sold under the hammer of Winstanley, the Liverpool auctioneer. Roscoe's books and manuscripts realised the sum of £5,150 and his paintings and drawings £5,875, making a total of £11,000.[12] Roscoe noted that his books probably fetched better prices than they would have in London.[13]

In his somewhat extravagant, though delightful, book on Roscoe's Library, James Aspinall tells us that Roscoe 'seems to have been positively embarrassed by the various intellectual treasures which he possessed and hardly to have known which to cultivate with the most decided devotion ... He appears to have had an appetite for everything, and generally with success. He went the tour of the arts, was at home in the sciences, made great advances in the classics and was as profound as he was enthusiastic in Italian history and literature.'[14] Certainly the catalogue drawn up by Roscoe, for the sale of his library, reflects the width of his interests. The books were classified according to their subject matter and the number of works in each section gives a rough indication of the extent of his interest in the various fields of learning.'[15] Roscoe's enthusiasm often outstripped his accuracy, as is evidenced by the fact that the majority of the attributions in his catalogue of a collection of his paintings, bought eventually for the Liverpool Institution, are believed to be incorrect.'[16]

Henry Roscoe tells us that his father's library, though not by any means as extensive as many private collections in England, was particularly rich in some of its departments.[17] The largest section of his library consisted of his collection of Italian poetry, made up of 343 works, including early editions of the works of Pulci and of Lorenzo de' Medici.

---

12   D.G. Weinglass, Publishing History of William Roscoe's edition of the Works of Alexander Pope, Esq. page 130, Record Office, Liverpool Central Library.

13   Holkham, M.S. 768, f.62.

14   'Roscoe's Library' by James Aspinall, 1853, page 70.

15   See the Appendix 1 which outlines the classification of Roscoe's library with the number of works sold in each category.

16   C,P Darcy, The Encouragement of the Fine Arts in Lancashire, 1760-1860. Darcy comments on page 60 on Roscoe's Catalogue of a Series of Pictures, illustrating the Rise and Early Progress of the Art of Painting in Italy, Germany, etc. (Liverpool, 1819).

17   Life of William Roscoe, by his son Henry, Vol.2, p.115.

He tells us that a copy of the 'Rappresentazione Sacri', which had cost his father a few shillings, sold for thirty guineas. His collection of classical authors, Latin and Greek, contained a number of first editions. One of Roscoe's favourite works was Dr T.F. Dibdin's 'Bibliomania, eight volumes, London, 1809, of which he was the possessor of the first and second editions.[18] Henry tell us that his father's taste for the study of bibliography led him into correspondence with Dibdin, whose magnificent volumes were frequently the subject of his admiration.[19] The principal collectors of books in Britain or their agents attended the sale and it is evident that the books, which aroused the greatest curiosity and interest were Roscoe's series of early printed books illustrating the rise and progress of the art of printing. Aspinall tells us:-

> 'there were many rare and valuable gems of literature and art, quaint old type suited to the quaint old phraseology, which it recorded, splendid trophies and monuments of early and late typography, books from the press of John Gutenberg, the Columbus of the art of printing, that glorious art which has given words, and wings, and vitality to thought and secured its fruits from the corroding power of time and oblivion.'[20]

At the end of the catalogue Roscoe added a list of 15th century printers whose productions appeared in his collection, together with the years in which they began to print. He also added a further list of the editions in his library which had escaped the notice of Panzer, the recognised authority on the earliest printed books, and whose work the 'Annales Typographici' was supposed to be a description of all printed books from the invention of the printing press to the year 1536.[21]

Roscoe's library contained two <u>block books</u> printed by Fust and Schoeffer before the invention by the latter of moveable type. It was Schoeffer who introduced the improvement of casting type in moulds.[22] These two rare books were the 'Historia S. Johannis' and the 'Biblia Pauperum, the Codex Psalmorum' or Psalter of 1459, which was the second book ever to be printed with a date, eight copies only of which

---

18 Life of William Roscoe, by his son Henry, Vol.2, p.115.

19 Dr Dibdin suggested to Roscoe that he write a Life of Erasmus. Roscoe in reply, wrote Such a work is much wanting, I admit, and I think it one of the finest subjects that could be undertaken; but you do me too much honour in thinking I am competent to it. Life of Wm. Roscoe by his son, Henry, Vol.ll, p.55.

20 Roscoe's Library, James Aspinall, 1853, page 30.

21 Life of Wm. Roscoe by his son, Henry, Vol.2, pages 116 and 117.

22 Roscoe's Library, James Aspinall, page 31.

were known to exist. There were also specimens of block-printing by its inventor, Laurence Coster.[23]

Another book of special interest contained the works of Lactantius, from the press of Sweynheyn and Pannartz, and was believed to be the first book printed in Italy, of such rarity that a celebrated bibliographer, De Bure, wrote there was only one copy known in France. The library contained a variety of other books from the printing presses of Italy, Germany and England, printed before 1500, among them volumes from the workshops of Sweynheyn, John de Spires, Husner, Creuzner, Drach, Wynkin de Worde, Richard Pynson, Aldus Manutius Romanus and others known to students of typography.[24]

After experimenting at Strasbourg for seventeen years with the use of cast letters and a press for printing, Gutenberg moved back to his home town, Mainz, and in partnership with Johannan Fust set up the first commercial printing press in 1445. H.A.L. Fisher tells us "'there was an immense enthusiasm for the new art' and quotes Wimpheling, a contemporary:- 'As the Apostles of Christianity formerly went through the world announcing the good news, so in our days the disciples of the new art spread themselves through all countries, and their books, heralds of the Gospel and the preachers of truth and science'".[25] Fisher goes on to say that printing from metal types reached Italy in 1465, Paris in 1470 and London in 1477 and that by the end of the century some nine million printed books must have been in existence 'as against a few score thousand manuscripts, which up to that time had contained the inherited wisdom and poetry of the world.'[26] Though a German invention, there were over a hundred printing presses in Italy by the end of 1500. Roscoe's library included examples from the early printing presses at Venice, Nicolas Jensen, 1470; Gabriele de Pietro, 1472; Theodore Reynsburch, 1477; at Boligno, John Neumeister, 1470; at Naples, Matthew Moravus, 1473; at Milan, Leonard Pachel, 1478; at Rome, Stephen Plannk, 1479; and at Florence, Antonio Miscomini, 1481.[27] For the first fifty years of the printing era much of the literature produced was theological, including more than a hundred editions of the Bible and fifty-nine of Thomas à Kempis' 'Imitation of Christ', partly due to the fact that clergy formed

---

23 Roscoe's Library, James Aspinall, Ch.IV, page 31.
24 Roscoe's Library, James Aspinall, Ch. IV, page 31.
25 History of Europe, 1936, H.A.L. Fisher, chapter 4, pp.465-6.
26 History of Europe, 1936, H.A.L. Fisher, chapter 4, pp.465-6.
27 George Chandler - Wm. Roscoe of Liverpool, page 107.

the greater part of the reading public. It is not surprising that many of Roscoe's most precious early printed works were of a religious nature.

James Aspinall claimed to be the proud possessor of a sale catalogue in which the price paid for each lot had been recorded in the margin.[28] Occasionally the buyer's name had also been mentioned. One book to which he draws special attention was the 'Catholicon' printed by John Gutenberg at Mainz in 1460, advertised as - 'a first edition yellow morocco, gilt leaves - a beautiful book in perfect condition, a gem', and sold for £63. After the sale of books, there followed the sale of manuscripts, one of which Aspinall described as the 'Koh-i-noor' of the collection - Lot 1800 - 'Biblia Sacra, utrumque Testamentum Vetus et Novum, veteri translatione ad Hebraicam et Graecam veritatum, continens Fol. MS on vellum, of the early part of the 14th century. This volume, Aspinall tells us, 'is decorated with historical designs from subjects of the Old and New Testament, supposed to be executed by Giotto, or some artist of his school: he having been employed at Avignon under Pope Clement V in 1305, about which time this manuscript was written. It appears to have been considered, at a subsequent period, as a present worthy of the supreme Pontiff, on which occasion a new frontispiece and the title page were added, illuminated with gold and colours. Besides the historical miniatures almost every page is decorated with arabesque ornaments, portraits, letters, etc. Independent of the value of this volume as exemplifying the state of art at a very early period, it is certainly one of the finest and most highly ornamented manuscripts of the sacred writings which has been handed down to the present times. The manuscript was bound in blue velvet, in a morocco case, by J. Jones of Liverpool, who had discovered a method of restoring the foldings in vellum leaves of ancient manuscripts to an equal surface, without injury to the writing.'[29] This precious manuscript was sold for £178-10s. to E. Rushton and G. Robinson. However correct or incorrect the attribution to Giotto and other historical details may be, there can be no doubt about Rocoe's love of ancient manuscripts, which prompted this poetic outburst:

> But when the studious hours decline,
>
> And tir'd attention wakes no more,
>
> Then, idly busy, be it mine
>
> Upon the pictur'd page to pore!

---

28   James Aspinall, Roscoe's Library, pages 35-36.

29   Aspinall, Roscoe's Library, Chapter IX, p.62.

Where rude designs of earlier days
   Their bright unchanging hues unfold,
And all th'illumin'd margins blaze
   With azure skies, and stars of gold;

Where on the solemn page intrude
   Figures grotesque, and emblems quaint,
And monsters of infernal brood
   Grin scornful at the preaching saint.

But see, where GIOTTO'S purer ray,
   Emerging from the gothic night,
Drives the fantastic shapes away,
   And brings his chaster forms to light.[30]

Perhaps the most precious of Roscoe's early Italian works was the 'Canzonieri of Petrarch', printed in Venice by Vindelinus de Spira in 1470. Roscoe is known to have bought his copy for £94-10s, a very high price in those days.[31] This book was sold at the bankruptcy sale. However Thomas Frater of Lorient presented him with another copy in 1824, as 'a signal recognition of his international reputation as a connoisseur of Italian civilisation'.[32] This presentation copy was bequeathed by the late Mrs A.M. Roscoe to the Picton Reference Library. The book was described by Dibdin as 'an extremely precious volume, among the most beautiful, as well as the rarest, of those executed by Vindelinus de Spira'.[33] Another of Roscoe's rare Italian books, purchased by his son, Henry, after his father's bankruptcy, 'De re aedificatoria' by Leo Baptista Alberti, is now in the Picton Reference Library. This book was printed in Florence by Nicolaus Laurentii, and is bound in blind

---

30 George Chandler, William Roscoe of Liverpool, page 107 et seq.

31 George Chandler, William Roscoe of Liverpool, page 108.

32 George Chandler, William Roscoe of Liverpool, page 108.

33 George Chandler, William Roscoe of Liverpool, page 108.

*Roscoe's youngest son, Henry 1800 - 1836,
the biographer of his father.*

tooled sheepskin. George Chandler, as City Librarian, bewailed the fact that such valuable books as the first folio Shakespeare and works from such early English printers as Wynkyn de Worde and Richard Pynson had left Liverpool - apparently for good.[34]

Henry Roscoe tells us that Lord Spencer, Mr Heber and other distinguished bibliographers were frequent purchasers at the sale.[35] On the recommendation of Roscoe, a number of books were bought on behalf of Mr Coke, as necessary additions to his library at Holkham.[36] George Chandler, writing in 1953, stated that some of Roscoe's books were among those recently acquired for the British Museum.[37] It was only after the sale of his library that Roscoe received a letter from the Rev. William Shepherd informing him that some of his friends in the Athenaeum Club had raised £600 to buy books likely to be useful 'in the correction of his standard works', presumably the Life of Lorenzo de' Medici and the Life and Pontificate of Leo X. After some hesitation, Roscoe refused to take them except on loan from the Athenaeum Club library, where they still remain to this day.[38]

34 Chandler, Wm. Roscoe of Liverpool, p.108.

35 Life of Wm. Roscoe, by his son, Henry, Vol.2, p.118.

36 Life of Wm. Roscoe, by his son, Henry, Vol.2, p.118.

37 G. Chandler, Wm. Roscoe of Liverpool, p.108.

38 Life of Wm. Roscoe, by his son Henry, Vol.2, page 121.

Chapter Six

Roscoe's Art Treasures

In 1824 Matthew Gregson, in his early days a publisher's agent for the sale of prints and later best known as an antiquarian, wrote to Roscoe suggesting that a record be made of the development of community patronage of art in Liverpool from 1760 onwards.[1] 'The first chapter would include a description of local print societies, a popular feature of social life in the latter part of the eighteenth century, whereby house groups were organised to purchase all the books and prints extant, to circulate them from house to house in rotation weekly, to collect the whole monthly, to meet and spend a pleasant evening over them; again to pass them around; at the end of the year to sell them amongst subscribers only and make fresh purchases again for the ensuing year. By this means the best and most expensive works have been in the possession of the Society and now remain divided amongst them.'[2] He goes on to describe a raffle for a print and then continues - 'A short while after this time I paid £18 for a print for your Brother in Law, Dan Daulby Esq. - and I paid 63 shillings for a portfolio to carry it in safety to Liverpool. The print was the Burgomaster Six by Rembrant ...'.[3]

This letter is significant because it reminds us of the surge of interest in prints during Roscoe's early days. It also testifies to the enthusiasm of Daniel Daulby as a collector of prints. On his death in 1797 Daulby left a large collection of books, prints and drawings and an interesting selection of the works of Old Masters and contemporary artists.[4] Roscoe followed eagerly in the footsteps of his brother-in-law in the formation of his own collection of art treasures and there is good reason to believe that Daniel Daulby was more knowledgeable and discerning as a

---

1   Matthew Gregson, Liverpool, 1824, Letter to William Roscoe, Roscoe Papers, Liverpool Record Office.

2   Matthew Gregson, Liverpool, 1824, Letter to William Roscoe, Roscoe Papers, Liverpool Record Office.

3   Matthew Gregson, Letter to William Roscoe, 1824, Roscoe Papers, Liverpool Record Office.

4   C.P. Darcy, The Encouragement of the Fine Arts in Lancashire 1760 to 1860 Manchester 1976, page 137.

connoisseur of fine art than Roscoe. Until Daulby's death Roscoe frequently sought his advice and thereafter relied chiefly upon Fuseli's guidance before buying works of art.

Godfrey Mathews, in his memoir of William Roscoe, published in 1931, to commemorate the centenary of his death, wrote 'It would be foolish to estimate Roscoe as a scientific historian and his credentials for engaging in this work might not pass with modern scholars.'[5] Edward Morris in an essay entitled 'Riches into Art' describes Roscoe as 'the last great exponent of that superficial school of art history which the distinguished art historian, Johann David Passavant, was about to render obsolete. He goes on to speak of Roscoe's approach to the history of art as that of preferring the broad sweep, rather than that of the specialist working in detail form primary resources.'[6] Roscoe was essentially an amateur in his published biographical and historical works as well as in his few writings on the progress of the arts. He became aware of his limitations as is made clear in his introduction to his Life of Leo X as also in his refusal to respond to publishers' requests for further historical works.[7] Roscoe may well have seemed more knowledgeable than in fact he was to his dilettanti friends and he may have been deluded by his admirers into thinking of himself as an art expert or as a worthy successor to Gibbon. Such delusions were not long lived.

Roscoe became acutely conscious of his deficiencies when he found himself in urgent need of help in completing a catalogue of his friend and patron Thomas Coke's valuable collection of illuminated manuscripts at Holkham in 1824. Frederic Madden, later to become keeper of manuscripts at the British Museum, came to the rescue, and having judged Roscoe's work to be valueless, proceeded to re-write the whole catalogue.[8] Morris describes this as 'the disaster of the Holkham manuscripts catalogue'. He goes on to tell us that 'Madden's new version was too long and too scholarly to have any appeal except to the expert'. Much to Madden's fury Coke refused to publish the new catalogue. Evidently Roscoe's friends and admirers including Coke, derived greater pleasure from Roscoe's chatty discursive and often inaccurate notes than from the writings of the pure scholar.

---

5   Godfrey W. Mathews, William Roscoe, 1913, London, page 27.

6   Edward Morris, Liverpool Historical Essays, Riches into Art, page 12.

7   Life of Wm. Roscoe by his son, Henry, Vol.2, pp.176-7.

8   Edward Morris, Liverpool Historical Essays, Riches into Art, pages 11 and 12.

Roscoe's contribution to the arts did not depend upon his accuracy or even upon his alleged inability to distinguish between a Flemish and Italian painting. It was founded upon his infectious and largely untutored interest in the arts, his own good taste and his comprehensive knowledge of art history made evident by many of his writings, not least of which was his Royal Institution inaugural lecture as chairman in 1817 'On the origin and Vicissitudes of Literature, Science and Art, and their Influence on the Present State of Society'. Above all else he is remembered for the practical steps he took to promote popular art education and the fact that an important part of his own collection is still available today for all to enjoy in the Walker Art Gallery in Liverpool.

It is not surprising that the catalogues of Roscoe's books and art treasures, drawn up by himself for the sale of his possessions following the bankruptcy, are often inaccurate and misleading. Their value lies only as an inventory of the items for sale and it is fortunate that some copies survive in the Liverpool Record Office in which the buyers' names and prices paid are marked in the margin. The catalogue is also useful because Roscoe outlines in the introduction the raison d'etre behind his collection, which was:

> 'chiefly for the purpose illustrating, by a reference to original and authentic sources, the rise and progress of the arts in modern times, as well in Germany and Flanders as in Italy. They are therefore not wholly to be judged by their positive merits, but by a reference to the age in which they were produced. Their value chiefly depends on their authenticity and the light they throw on the history of the arts'[9]

Morris speaks of Roscoe's collection as 'his slide library'.[10] Roscoe appears to have been more devastated by the loss of his books than of his art treasures. Many of the latter he had in his possession only for a short time before the collapse of his bank. He wrote a moving sonnet to mark the loss of his books, which he regarded as his friends.[11] There was no poem to commemorate his parting with the art treasures, which he accepted with resignation, clinging to the hope that they would remain in Liverpool for posterity.

---

9   Wm. Roscoe, Catalogue of the Genuine and Entire Collection of Drawings and Pictures, the Property of William Roscoe, 1816. Liverpool Record Office.

10   Edward Morris, Liverpool Historical Essays, Riches into Art, page 18.

11   William Roscoe - Sonnet on Parting with his Books - see chapter 1, page 45.

The sale of Roscoe's art treasures followed the sale of his books and was divided into two parts. The first eleven days, beginning on Monday, September 9th 1816 were devoted to the disposal of his massive collection of prints and etchings. The second part lasting a further six days consisted of the sale of his original drawings and paintings. The first part of the catalogue, all of which was prepared by Roscoe himself and which ran to a hundred and seventy pages, comprised 1394 lots described as follows:

'A series of prints from the works of the Greek and Italian painters, illustrative of the progress of painting in Italy, from the earliest to the later ages'.

A series of prints illustrative of the progress of engraving in Italy, Germany, and Flanders: including choice specimens of every artist of eminence, from the earliest period to Agostino Caracci, in the Italian school; and from Francis Stoss to Edelinck, in the German and Flemish.

A highly valuable collection of etchings, by the Italian painters, consisting of the works of the most eminent masters, who had etched their own designs, from Parmigiano to Carlo Maratti. Of the Flemish and Dutch painters in various walks of history, landscape, cattle, drolls and interiors; and of the French School including fine examples of Claude, Callot, Gaspar Poussin, Sebastian Bourdon, etc.

An assemblage of fine prints, after Rubens, by the most celebrated engravers of his time. Choice impressions of the Vandyke heads. Several fine works of Rembrandt and his school. Rare specimens of wood and chiar-scuro prints by the Italian and German masters. Engravings from antique busts and statues, a few select books of prints, etc.'

The collection of prints and etchings yielded the sum of £1,915-1s. This part of the sale attracted more public interest than the sale of old masters and artists' drawings which followed it. Print collecting had become a popular pastime among people of moderate means. Apart from dealers there were two or three substantial buyers including C. Blundell, but the bulk of the purchasers, among them many of Roscoe's friends and acquaintances, contented themselves with one or two bargains. The result was that his collection of prints was widely dispersed.

The more valuable part of his collection, comprising old masters and drawings had for the most part been purchased by Roscoe during the first fifteen years of the nineteenth century, when he was at the height of his prosperity. He patronised dealers in London and Liverpool. In London he did business with Thomas Philipe, who in 1795 sent him a consignment, described as a shipment, of art works on approval. This was dispatched by post coach to Birchfield. In a covering note Philipe stated that - 'the above articles are sent to you for your amusement, and if they in any degree answer the purpose, you may have frequent parcels in the same way.'[12]

Roscoe duly returned items not required and paid for the rest. Further correspondence indicates that from time to time Philipe acted as agent for Roscoe in London.[13]

Roscoe relied less on Philipe after the establishment in business at Liverpool around the turn of the century of Thomas Winstanley as a dealer, who handled Old Masters and contemporary works, but specialised in the early schools of art. C.P. Darcy expressed the opinion that it is impossible to tell whether Winstanley had any influence on the taste of Roscoe, but reminds us that the date of his arrival in Liverpool coincided exactly with the date at which Roscoe began to collect most actively.[14] What is certain is that Winstanley played a leading part in enabling Roscoe to build up his historical collection, supplying him with more than fifty important pictures.

Henry Roscoe tells us that 'a considerable number of the pictures, which though highly curious as illustrating the history of art, were little interesting to the ordinary collector, and did not meet with purchasers at the sale.'[15] This may at the time seem to have been something of a disappointment, but it turned out in the end to be the best thing which could possibly have happened for the people of Liverpool. Three pictures, which Henry describes as the flowers of the collection, were purchased by Mr Coke of Holkham through an agent, Mr Arch, who represented him at the sale. These were the Madonna and Child with St. Helena and St. Francis by Ghirlandaio, with a frieze by Michelangelo, A Head of Christ by Leonardo da Vinci and Andrea de Sarto's copy of a portrait of

---

12 Thomas Philipe, London 14th January 1795 - letter to Wm. Roscoe - Roscoe Papers 2961, Liverpool Record Office.

13 See also correspondence - Roscoe Papers 2962 to 2966, Liverpool Record Office.

14 C.P. Darcy, The encouragement of the Fine Arts in Lancashire 1760-1860, Manchester 1976, page 127.

15 Life of Wm. Roscoe, by his son Henry, Vol.2, page 139.

Pope Leo X.[16] He bought three other items at the sale; Giorgione's Lady, Lovin's Vergin and Child and the Tortelli Commentaria, paying the sum of £1,229.5.10 for these six works. It is thought that Mr Coke bought these works of art, as well as £400 worth of books out of sympathy with Roscoe in his misfortune and also to enable him to enjoy them on his visits to Holkham Hall.

Roscoe would have much preferred to see them form part of a public collection for all to see in Liverpool than to remain in private hands. The prime object of his collection was that it be used for educational purposes to promote an interest in the fine arts and the history of art among the whole community.

Reference is made to two of these precious pictures in a review of Winstanley's Observations on the Arts, which appeared in the Liverpool Chronicle in 1829.[17]

'For more than thirty years he (Winstanley) has been actively engaged in the buying and selling of pictures, during which period some of the finest works of the Kingdom have passed through his hands. Two instances illustrative of this assertion, deserve to be placed on record. During the short peace in 1802, led by his favourite pursuit, the author visited Paris, where he purchased the Head of our Saviour, painted by Leonardo da Vinci, which was so long a distinguished ornament of the collection at Allerton. The head was sold by Mr Winstanley to Mr Roscoe for forty guineas; and at the sale of the splendid collection at Allerton, it was sold to Mr Coke of Norfolk for 300 guineas. The picture of Leo and his Cardinals, after Raffaelle, and del Sarto, was also bought by Mr Winstanley for Mr Roscoe for less than half the price Mr Coke gave for it at the same sale'. Few of Roscoe's explanatory notes in his catalogue, prepared by himself for the sale of his paintings are to be relied upon, but it is hard to believe that the story behind what was then regarded as the most valuable and remarkable picture in his collection is apocryphal. The story behind this copy of Raphael's portrait of Pope Leo X, with his cousin, the Cardinal Giulio de'Medici and his nephew, the Cardinal de Rossi, is interesting:-[18]

---

16 Roscoe Papers 918 - Account for books bought at the sale by Mr Arch on behalf of Mr Coke, November 15th 1 816.

17 The Liverpool Chronicle, January 24th 1829, page 26.

18 Life of William Roscoe by his son Henry, Volume 2, pages 130 **et seq. and the** Catalogue of the Drawings and Pictures, the Property of William Roscoe, Liverpool, 1816.

'Vasari relates, that when Federigo, Duke of Mantua, passed through Florence, to pay his respects to Clement Vll, he saw in the palace of the Medici the portrait of Leo X, with the Cardinals Giulio de Medici and Rossi, with which he was so highly pleased, that on his arrival at Rome he requested it as a gift from the Pope, who then was at the head of the Medici family and one of the persons represented in the picture. The Pontiff generously complied with his wishes, and directions were accordingly sent to Ottaviano de'Medici at Florence to forward the picture to Mantua; but he being unwilling that the family should be deprived of such a treasure, sent to Andrea del Sarto and requested him to copy it, which he did with such success, that Ottaviano himself could not distinguish the copy from the original; concealing, therefore the picture of Raffaelle, he sent to Mantua that of Andrea del Sarto, with which the Duke was perfectly satisfied, and even Giulio Romano, the favourite pupil of Raffaelle, who was then at Mantua, was not aware of the deception.

'In his error they might have remained, had not a singular accident led to an explanation. Vasari, then a young and rising artist, desirous of forming an acquaintance with Giulio Romano, paid a visit to Mantua,where he was received with great civility by Giulio, who, after gratifying him with a sight of the works of art which the city afforded, at length exhibited to him the picture of Raffaelle, as the greatest ornament of the place. 'A beautiful work!' cried Vasari 'but not by the hand of Raffaelle.' - 'How so?' said Giulio. 'Is it possible I should not recognise the touches of my own pencil upon it?' - 'You are mistaken', replied Vasari: 'this picture is the work of Andrea del Sarto' (under whom Vasari had studied at the time the copy was made); 'and as a proof of it, there is a mark on it which I will show you.' The picture was accordingly taken down, and the mark mentioned by Vasari discovered; upon which Giulio declared, 'that he valued the copy no less than the picture of Raffaelle himself; nay' he added, 'even more because it is incredible that one painter should so perfectly imitate the manner of another.'

In consequence of this artifice the picture of Raffaelle remained at Florence, till it was carried away a few years since to ornament the immense collection of the Louvre; that of Andrea del Sarto afterwards came into the possession of the Duke of Parma, from which city it was transferred to Naples, and formed a part of the royal collection at Capo di Monte, where it remained till that collection was dispersed by the revolutionary troubles, and is presumed to have found its way, in common with many other pictures of the same collection, in to this country, where it became the property of a respectable dealer in London, who never would part with it in his lifetime, but after whose death it was purchased by its present possessor (William Roscoe).

During the time these pictures were in Italy, they were the frequent subject of comparison and criticism. Richardson, in his account of the works of art in Italy, (vol. iii, p.665) says, there are those who pretend that the copy is preferable to the original, but to judge properly it would be requisite to see them together. He prefers the original, but at the same time he doubts whether he may not be prejudiced in favour of Raffaelle. The prelate Bottari, the learned editor and annotator of Vasari's Lives of the Painters, relates that by particular favour he obtained a sight of the picture at Naples, (about the year 1756) and returned twice to examine it, but could not obtain permission to take it out of the frame. 'I can however say', adds he 'that this is one of the most stupendous pictures I have ever seen, and appears not to have been painted more than six months. I have fresh in my memory the original of Raffaelle, which I saw not many years since, and I aver that, setting aside the names of the painters and the knowledge of the facts, many good judges would take the copy in preference to the original, which is now turned rather black; whilst the copy, besides its freshness, is more soft and fleshy than the original'.

Roscoe gives further evidence to support the contention that the picture on sale was in fact Andrea del Sarto's copy of Raphael's masterpiece.[19] Yet another copy of Raphael's painting may be found in the Corsini Gallery, a copy with a difference. In it figures of Pope Leo X and his cousin Giulio, the future Pope Clement Vll are the same as in the original, but the black bearded Cardinal Cibo Bugiardini has taken the place of the clean shaven Cardinal Luigi de Rossi standing behind the chair.[20]

19 Life of Wm. Roscoe by his son Henry, Vol.2, pp.134-6.
20 John Burchard's Diaries (London 1910) translated by A.H. Matthews, page 336.

Giovanni de Lorenzo de'Medici, Pope Leo X, portrayed by Raphael with the Pope's cousin, Giulio, the future Pope Clement VII, on his right and Cardinal Luigi de' Rossi standing behind the chair.

Henry Roscoe appears to have given a misleading and oversimplified account of the dispersal of his father's art treasures, when he stated that after the sale the same gentlemen, who bought a number of books from his library and presented them to the Liverpool Athenaeum, purchased 'a series of specimens of the Italian and German Schools and gave them to the Liverpool Royal Institution'.[21] It appears that Roscoe and his friends, anxious about the possible outcome of the sale and determined to keep the paintings in Liverpool, at a private meeting held before the sale contrived a plan to save the situation. Disregarding what was said in the catalogue about 'without reserve', Roscoe himself bought secretly through local dealers a large part of his historical collection at the sale itself, valued by Winstanley at 1553 guineas.[22] He proceeded to offer it to the Liverpool Royal Institution at the bargain price of 1200 guineas. The offer must have been turned down for lack of funds or through lack of interest. Consequently Roscoe and his friends decided to launch a public appeal to cover the cost of the paintings in order to present them as an outright gift to the Institution. In a letter sent in June 1818, nearly two years after the sale, to Dr Traill, Roscoe wrote with cautious optimism about the public appeal:-[23] 'I shall think myself sufficiently gratified if the liberality of my townsmen shall so far second my wishes to prevent a collection formed with a view to public utility from being dispersed'. The appeal proved a success; the collection was bought by public subscription and was given to the Liverpool Royal Institution. Apart from this, Roscoe managed to retain a group of carefully selected primitives including real masterpieces as well as pictures from other periods. These he sold to the Institution at a later date.[24] It was a credit to the people of Liverpool that, despite their early suspicion of Roscoe's 'curious taste in art, they did acquire his valuable collection for permanent public display.

---

21 Life of Wm. Roscoe by his son Henry, Vol.2, page 140.

22 C.P. Darcy, The Encouragement of the Fine Arts in Lancashire, Manchester 1976, page 60.

23 William Roscoe, Liverpool, June 16, 1818, Letter to Dr Traill, Roscoe Papers 486 A, Liverpool Record Office.

24 C.P. Darcy, Encouragement of the Fine Arts in Lancashire, page 60. A detailed account of the formation of the Liverpool Royal Institution Art Gallery, its purpose and content, may be found by Edward Morris in the Transactions of the Historic Society of Lancashire and Cheshire, 1992, pp.87-97.

Henry Fuseli, 1741-1825,
with whom Roscoe corresponded 1783-1821.
Fuseli admired Roscoe's Poem on Burke.
After an oil painting by John Williamson in the Roscoe Collection,
Walker Art Gallery, Liverpool

Those of Roscoe's collection of paintings which were saved from
dispersal as a result of a public appeal and a number of others sold direct
to the Liverpool Royal Institution, were kept and displayed at the Institution
from 1819 until 1893. A new purpose built art gallery was constructed
adjacent to the Institution's main premises in Colquitt Street in 1844. In
1850 negotiations took place between the Liverpool Royal Institution and
the Liverpool Town Council, which had been authorised by Parliament to
provide museums and art galleries at the expense of the ratepayers. The
Institute wanted to retain some control over its art collection and this led
to a breakdown in the negotiations. By 1860 plans were made for the
establishment of a new public art gallery. Little progress was made until a
wealthy brewer, Andrew Barclay Walker, Mayor of Liverpool, made a
contribution of £20,000 towards the erection of a public art gallery, later
adding an additional £11,500 towards an enlargement. The Walker Art
Gallery was completed and opened to the public in 1877. It was used not
only for art exhibitions but for its growing permanent collection. By 1882
Liverpool was the proud possessor of the finest art gallery outside London.
In 1893 the Liverpool Royal Institution decided to hand over the paintings
on long term loan for display at the Walker Art Gallery. It was not until
1948 that the Liverpool Royal Institution finally presented outright to the
Walker Art Gallery the paintings already on loan.

A number of Fuseli's best works formed a part of Roscoe's collection,
some of which had been painted at his request. Fuseli, having spent
eight years studying art in Italy, returned to London determined to
emulate Michaelangelo's 'manifestations of the SUBLIME',[25] not
without a measure of success. With Roscoe's financial support Fuseli
opened the 'Milton Gallery' in Pall Mall in 1790 with an exhibition of
forty-seven of his paintings.[26] Fourteen years later Fuseli was elected
Professor of Painting at the Royal Academy. Roscoe and Fuseli became
close friends, Roscoe benefitting from Fuseli's knowledge of art and Fuseli
relying on Roscoe's patronage. Fuseli, an admirer and friend of William
Blake, allowed his imagination to run riot, deliberately exploiting the
horrific and fantastic. Roscoe encouraged the marketing of Fuseli's work
in the north and described it as the 'experiment of Liverpool'.[27] A number of

---

25 The Oxford Companion to Art, Fuseli, Henry, page 449.

26 C.P. Darcy, The Encouragement of the Fine Arts in Lancashire, 1976, page 137.

27 Hugh MacAndrew, Henry Fuseli and William Roscoe. The Liverpool Bulletin, Vll -
    1959-60, p.52.

Roscoe's friends were persuaded with some difficulty to buy some of Fuseli's works. Though not popular during his life-time, Fuseli's paintings appealed later in the nineteenth century to the imagination of the Impressionists and Surrealists. Roscoe appreciated Fuseli's work and his dining-room at Allerton was entirely decorated with his paintings. Pride of place was given to a large painting of 'the Death of Lorenzo de' Medici' which hung above the fire-place - on a canvass of six feet by nearly five. This picture was intended to illustrate Roscoe's graphic description of Lorenzo's death-bed scene in chapter ten of his biography. Fuseli and Roscoe devoted much time and thought to the posture of the subjects and the expression on their faces. Fuseli asked Roscoe to send him some kind of visual representation of Lorenzo, Politiano and Pico. Roscoe sent what he could lay hands on and received Fuseli's reply: "The medals and print your son left with me are, with regard to Lorenzo, abominable caricatures; do not suffice to Pico, and turn Politiano into a fat schoolmaster. It will therefore be some merit to have done better, and yet to have preserved some likeness. After all, I suspect, between you and me, your hero to have been an ill-looking fellow! The head of Attila, as we find on medals, has elevation and beauty compared with the human reptile you sent me. Pico, on the medal, has an air of age beyond what he attained, and looks not very unlike Mr Whitbread.'[28] This picture was destined to haunt Roscoe and his family for many years. A purchaser, who wished to remain anonymous bought the picture at the sale, requesting the auctioneer, Mr Winstanley, to hand it over to Roscoe, who directed that after his death it be presented to the Liverpool Athenaeum,[29] where it was kept for a number of years, but no trace of it can now be found.

Roscoe's historical collection of paintings is described in the Walker Art Gallery Foreign Catalogue as 'the first notable collection of Old Master Paintings bought in order to improve public taste'. The illustrated popular 'Guide to Pictures in the Walker Art Gallery' gives pride of place to Simone Martini's painting from Roscoe's collection - 'Christ Discovered in the Temple'.[30] It is one of the earliest paintings in the gallery. The artist inscribed his name and the date in the gold frame:- 'Simone of Siena painted me in 1342'. This painting is the last dated work of Simone and the only dated work extant from his Avignon period.[31]

---

28 Life of William Roscoe by his son, Henry, Vol.2, pages 138 and 139.
29 Life of William Roscoe by his son, Henry, Vol.2, pages 138 and 139.
30 Pictures in the Walker Art Gallery, 1980, page 16.
31 Walker Art Gallery, Foreign Catalogue-Text (1977), p.114.

It is interesting also because it is unusual, illustrating an incident in the gospel story rarely portrayed by artists. The title might well have been 'Misunderstanding in the Holy Family'. Mary, scolding Jesus for his disappearance, asks, 'Why hast thou thus dealt with us? Behold thy father and I have sought thee sorrowing'. Jesus replied, arms folded, with complete assurance and without a trace of defiance, 'Wist ye not that I must be about my father's business?' - a question which Mary and Joseph were unable to answer at that time. Simone tells us that the Holy family was a real family made up of real people facing real problems.

Another outstanding specimen from the Roscoe collection is the Pieta by Ercole de Roberti of the Ferrarese school - originally part of a set of small panels placed below an Italian altar-piece. This moving picture, stark in its simplicity, represents the Virgin mourning over the dead Christ with the Crucifixion painted sketchily in a hazy distance in the background. 'In this painting we are invited to share her grief, and to feel outrage at the Crucifixion'.[32]

Jan Mostaert's 'Portrait of a Young Man' - c 1520 - is not only a specially interesting picture; it is also a key painting in Roscoe's historical collection, marking a transitional phase in Netherlandish art, as the influence of the Italian Renaissance was making itself felt in northern Europe. Mostaert was appointed painter to Margaret of Austria, Regent of the Netherlands, and accompanied her on her travels making portraits of her courtiers.

This complex picture consists of two paintings - the portrait itself of a smartly dressed, thoughtful and perhaps rather sad young man, and a background depicting the legend of St. Hubert,[33] the patron saint of huntsmen, including numerous scenes - a walled town, a picnic, two whippets reflected in the water as they drink, a swan, a groom and huntsman with horn. The young man is kneeling in prayer on a dry stone dyke, using it as a prie-dieu. It is possible that the young man's name is Hubert and that he has a special interest in his patron saint. However there is a 'Portrait of a Woman' by Mostaert in the Rijkmuseum (Inv. No. 1674A1) with exactly the same background.[34] Both of the sitters may have belonged to a confraternity dedicated to St. Hubert.

---

32 Pictures in the Walker Art Gallery, Merseyside County Council, 1980, page 18.

33 'Pictures in Walker Art Gallery, Liverpool', 1980 page 24. "St Hubert went out hunting on a holy day when such activities were forbidden. The stag he was chasing suddenly turned round and Hubert saw that it had a crucifix between its horns: confronted with this miracle he fell on his knees to worship it and to repent of his sin."

34 Walker Art Gallery, Foreign Catalogue, page 136.

One of the paintings Roscoe treasured most, now entitled St Bernardino Preaching, was bought at the sale in 1816 by Dr Traill, who would often have seen it on visits to Roscoe's house and would have known how much it meant to him. Dr Traill presented it to the Liverpool Royal Institution in 1819, despite the fact that Thomas Coke of Norfolk had written to Roscoe a few days before the sale expressing an interest in acquiring it.[35] The painting is now thought to have come from the studio of Pietro di Lorenzo Vecchietta, though there is no absolute certainty about this. In 1810 it was described as 'A Congregation' by Masaccio. The preacher is St Bernardino of Siena (1380-1440) known to have cultivated the veneration of the Holy Name and to have held up during his sermons a tablet inscribed with the initials IHS as in the picture. The church is unrecognisable in Florence or elsewhere, but may have been that of San Francesco, Siena, which was destroyed by fire in 1655.[36] Roscoe deluded himself into thinking that the church was the cathedral at Florence and that the family party approaching from the south side consisted of Cosimo de Medici with his son Piero, preceded by Lorenzo

Roscoe believed this to be a true image of the Medici family,
Lorenzo and Giuliano followed by their father
Piero and their grandfather Cosimo de' Medici.

---

35   Roscoe Papers 912, Liverpool Record Office, Letter from Coke to Roscoe - September 1816.

36   Walker Art Gallery, Liverpool, Foreign Catalogue Text pages 212 and 213 St. Bernardino Preaching 2758.

aged twelve and his younger brother Giuliano, followed by a retinue of relatives and dependents. Roscoe believed the picture to have been painted by Francesco Pesellino, an Italian painter of the Florentine School known to have been employed by Cosimo de Medici.

Roscoe, six years after the sale of his paintings took the trouble to include in his book 'Illustrations Historical and Critical of the Life of Lorenzo de Medici' a print copied from the original painting, which he was convinced was a true, almost photographic, image of the Medici family. He commented upon the fact that Piero's infirmities were strikingly apparent and that the family was all dressed in the costume of the time.[37] The evidence suggests that all this was a figment of Roscoe's vivid imagination. If this is so it would be good to discover the identity of this unknown family party.

There follows, in the Appendix II a list of paintings, all of which formed a part of Roscoe's historical collection, permanently housed in the Walker Art Gallery, and all described in the Foreign Catalogue. These pictures survive as an enduring reminder of William Roscoe, to whose vision, energy and enthusiasm the people of Liverpool owe so much.

---

37 William Roscoe, Illustrations Historical and Critical of the Life of Lorenzo de'Medici, London and Edinburgh 1822, pages 89 et seq.

Roscoe of Liverpool

Appendix I

The sale by auction of William Roscoe's Library at Liverpool began on Monday, August 19th 1816 and lasted a fortnight. The books were classified and sold in the following order:

The Art of Deciphering Manuscripts	8 works
Typography, 13: Bibliography	27 works
Libraries, Collections, etc.	37 works
Treatises on Languages, Grammars, Dictionaries	58 works
Criticism, Literary Journals	68 works
Literary, History and Biography	61 works
History and Chronology	17 works
Grecian History, 23: Roman History	37 works
Italian History, 78: French History, 15: English History	37 works
History of Various Nations, Voyages and Travels - Voyages and Travels - Kashmir, China, Persia, Africa, Ethiopia, Siam, Japan, Tartaria, East Indies	25 works
Ecclesiastical, 32: Theology and Controversial Divinity	74 works
Moral Philosophy, 51: Philosophy, Metaphysics	46 works
Letters, Orations etc. 74: Greek Poets,	80 works
Latin Poets, 52: Modern Latin Poets	60 works
ITALIAN POETS, 343: French Poets	43 works
ENGLISH POETS	129 works
Romances, Facetiae, Fables, Satires	126 works
Ancient Art, 22: Didactic and Critical Works on Art	28 works
Lives of Painters, 29: Collections and Catalogues of Pictures, Drawings and Prints,	32 works

Natural History, 95 works - followed by some manuscripts, Latin, Italian, French and English, some sacred writings and a few assorted books omitted in Roscoe's catalogue.

Roscoe of Liverpool

Appendix II

	Central Italian School, early 16th century
2866	Adoration of the Magi

	Ercole de Roberti - active 1479, died 1496
2773	Pieta

	Fabritius, Carel, 1622-1654
959	Portrait of a Bearded man

	Florentine School c.1480-90
2809	Adventures of Odysseus

	Florentine School, 17th century
2840	Mythological Figure

	French School, about 1500
1315	Lamentation over the Dead Christ

	French School, about 1530
1308	Portrait of a Lady with a Parrot

	French School, late 18th century
1309	Head of an Old Man

	Isenbrandt, Adriaen, active 1510, died 1551
1017	Virgin and Child

	Italian School, 17th century
2991	Portrait of a man

	Kneller, Godfrey, after
2537	Matthew Prior

	Krell, Hans c.1522-1586
1222	Portrait of Princess Emilia of Saxony (1516-1591)

	Martini, Simone, c.1284-1344
2787	Christ discovered in the Temple

Master of the Virgo inter Virgines, active 1480-1495
1014   The Entombment

Michaelangelo Buonarotti, 1475-1564
2789   Christ and the Woman of Samaria

Mostaert, Jan 1475-1555
1018   Portrait of a Young Man

Netherlandish School, late 15th century
1186   Christ Nailed to the Cross

1021   Rest on the Flight into Egypt

Netherlandish School, 16th century
873   Martyrdom of St. Lawrence
818   Prodigal Son
1013   St. Catherine
1016   The Nativity
1188   Portrait of a Merchant
1193   The Nativity

Netherlandish School, early 17th century
834   The Murder of Abel

North Italian School c.1550
1187   A Warrior Saint in a red cuirass holding a spear

North Italian School c.1600
      Set of Portraits of Famous Men and Women, 39 survive - one missing - mostly copies collected by Paolo Giovio, bishop of Nocera (1483-1552).

Perugino, Pietro, 1445-1523
2856   The Birth of the Virgin
2797   Head of a Woman
2890   Madonna and Child with St John and three angels

Roman School about 1700
2858   Death of Lucretia

Rosselli, Cosimo, 1439-1507
2803   A martyr Saint, probably St. Lawrence

Rosso Fiorentio, 1495-1540
2804   Portrait of a Young Man with Helmet

Schongauer, Martin, 1430-1491, after
1015   Agony in the Garden

Spanish School, 16th century
1180   Pietà

Spinello Aretino, 1373-1410
2752   Salome

2753   The Infant John presented to Zacharias

Tintoretto, Jacobo Robusti 1518-1594 after
2850   The Last Judgement

Vecchietta, Pietro di Lorenzo, studio of 1410-1480
2758   St. Bernardino Preaching

Vincentino, Andrea Michieli, 1539-1614
2847   The Court of Heaven

Bandinelli, Baccio, 1493-1560 studio of
2137   Six figures seated around a fire
1458   Nude man Kneeling

Bartholommeo di Giovanni (active 1485-1510), Florence,
2756   A Legend of St. Andrew

Bartolommeo, Fra, 1472-1517
8698   Madonna adoring the Christ Child - other side,
     Creation of Eve

Boucher, Francois, 1703-1770, after
2517   Three Putti in Clouds

Brueghel, Jan the elder, 1568-1625
6352   The Crossing of the Red Sea by the Israelites
and the Destruction of Pharaoh's Armies

Claude Gellee, 1600-1682
6176   Study of trees with two figures

French School, 18th century
6617   Isaiah showing Hezekiah the shadow on the Dial

Grimaldi, Giovanni Francesco, 1606-1680
6169   Landscape with Figures beside a River

Guercino, ll, Barbieri, Giovanni Francesco, 1591-1666
9213   A Monstrous Animal and a Peasant

Moyaert, Claes Cornelisz c.1600-1669
6939   The Return of Tobit

North Italian School, late 16th century
4160   The Holy Family with St. Elizabeth and
St. John the Baptist and angels

Parmigianino
4161   Three Figures after an Antique refief

Passarotti, Bartolommeo, 1529-1592
8467   Portrait of Giovanni II Bentivoglio

Polidoro da Caravaggio, 1499-1543 after
4159   Figures from a frieze

Salviati, Francesco dei Rossi, 1510-1563
6171   Study for an allegorical female figure

Silvestro dei Gherarducci, Don, 1352-1399
2764   The Birth of St. John the Baptist

Stradano, Jan van der Straet, 1523-1605
6312   The Prophet Micah

Tamagni da San Gimignano, Vicenzo, 1492-1538
4162   A woman with a distaff

Waterloo, Athonie, 1609-1690
6172   A wood at the side of a river

Zucchi, Jacopo, 1541-1589
6558   Pope Leo X blessing King Francis I of France

From Catalogue of Prints

Abbate, Niccolo dell' 1509-1571
9124   Two Roman Women

Beccafumi, Domenico 1486-1551 after
9123   The four doctors of the church

Bonasone, Giulio after Carrucci, Jacobo, 1531-1574
9184   The Birth of St. John the Baptist

Bourdon, Sebastien 1616-1671
9170   The Holy Family with the infant
         St. John the Baptist and a bird, probably
         a goldfinch symbolising the Passion
9171   The Holy Family with the Infant
         St John the Baptist (La Vierge à l'ecuelle)
9172   The Flight into Egypt

Carracci, Annibale, 1560-1609
9190   Christ Mocked
9191   The Adoration of the Shepherds

Carracci, Annibale, after
9121   Christ and the Samaritan Woman at the Well

Carracci, Lodovico, 1555-1619
9188   The Madonna and Child with the
          infant Saint John the Baptist

Carracci, Lodovico, after
9189   The Madonna and Child with the
          infant St. John the Baptist

Clouwet, Albertus, 1636-1679
8569   Portrait of Baccio Bandinelli

Fantuzzi, Antonio, active 1537-1550 after Rosso Fiorentino
9119   Contest between Minerva and Neptune

Franco, Giovanni Battista, 1498-1561
9185   Melchisedech offering bread and wine to Abraham

Giordano, Luca, 1632-1705
9174   The Assumption and Coronation of Saint Anne

Grimaldi, Giovanni Francesco, 1606-1680
9186   The rest on the Flight from Egypt
9187   The two goats

Mannozzi, Giovanni, 1592-1636 after
9175   An allegorical subject

Palma, Jacopo, 1544-1628
9179   Allegorical figure of Rome holding a statuette of Victory
9180   Holy Family with St. Francis and Jerome
9181   Christ and the woman taken in adultery
9182   Studies of ten heads, two backs, one torso, etc.

Palma, Jacopo, after
9183   The Adoration of the Shepherds

Raimondi, Marcantonio c.1480-1527 after
4164   Venus and Cupid

Reni,Guido, 1575-1642
9120   The Holy Family

Reni, Guido after Carracci, Lodovico, 1555-1619
9192   The Adoration of the Magi

Rode, Christian Bernhard, 1725-1797
9168   Frederick William the Great Elector riding a sleigh
           about to cross the Frisches Haff with his infantry

Rosa, Salvator, 1615-1 673
9169   Alexander the Great in the Studio of Apelles

Rossigliani, Guiseppe Nicola early 16th century after
Parmagianino

9177   The Adoration of the Magi
           Veneziano, Agostino dei Musi 1490 - still active 1536

4163   Hercules strangling the serpents

Bibliography

Books and Other Writings
by William Roscoe

1770   "Select Poems from Several Authors". 4 volumes Manuscripts

1774   "An Ode on the Institution of a Society in Liverpool for the Encouragement of Designing, Drawing, Painting, etc." Liverpool.

1777   "Mount Pleasant, a descriptive Poem" Liverpool.

1787   "The Wrongs of Africa, a Poem", Part 1, London.

1788   "A General View of the African Slave-trade, demonstrating its injustice and impolicy with Hints towards a Bill for its Abolition" London.

1788   The Wrongs of Africa, a Poem, Part 2, London.

1788   "A Scriptural Refutation of a Pamphlet, lately published by the Rev. Raymond Harris entitled: 'Scriptural Researches on the licitness of the Slave-trade', London.

1789   "Ode to the People of France". Liverpool.

1790   "The Dingle" Liverpool.

1791   "The Life, Death and Wonderful Achievements of Edmund Burke. A new ballad" Liverpool.

1791   "The Day-star of Liberty". Liverpool Broadsheet.

1791   "Poesie del Magnifico Lorenzo de'Medici, tratte da testi a penna della Libreria Mediceo-Laurenziana e finora inedite". Liverpool. Also incorporated in successive editions of his Life of Lorenzo de'Medici.

1792   An Inquiry into the Causes of the Insurrection of the Negroes in the Island of St. Domingo". London.

1793   "Thoughts on the Causes of the present Failures" London.

1795   Edward Rogers of Everton, Liverpool. Broadsheet.

1795   "The Life of Lorenzo de'Medici, called the Magnificent" 2 volumes Liverpool- followed by five further editions in London during his life-time and four after his death, as well as editions in France, Germany, Italy, Greece and in America.

1796   Strictures on Mr Burke's two Letters addressed to a member of the present Parliament, London.

1796   "Observations on the Works of Rembrandt", prefixed to Daniel Daulby's 'Descriptive Catalogue of the Works of Rembrandt'" Liverpool.

1798   "The Nurse, a Poem. Translated from the Italian of Luigi Tansillo" Liverpool, 2nd edition 1800: 3rd ed. 1804.

1802   "An Address delivered before the Proprietors of the Botanic Garden in Liverpool" previous to the opening of the Garden on May 3rd, 1802, to which are added the laws of the institution and a list of proprietors.

1802   "Observations on the relative situation of Great Britain and France" Liverpool.

1803   "The Metrical Miscellany" including eight poems by Roscoe, 2nd edition, London.

1805   "The Life and Pontificate of Leo X" 4 volumes, Liverpool. Five further editions in London, also editions in Paris, in Leipzig and Vienna and in Milan.

1807   "The Butterfly's Ball and the Grasshopper's Feast, Liverpool.

1808   "Considerations on the Causes, Objects and Consequences of the present War, etc." London.

1808   "Remarks on the Proposals made to Great Britain for opening negotiations for Peace in the year 1807". London.

1809   "The Butterfly's Birthday", London.

1809   Preface to the 'British Gallery of Contemporary Portraits' - London.

1810   "Brief Observations on the Address to His Majesty proposed by Earl Grey in the House of Lords, June 13, 1810. Liverpool

1810   A Paper on Farm Leases read before the Agricultural Society of West Derby, Liverpool.

1811   "A Reply to some Remarks by George Harrison on a Communication from William Roscoe to the Duke of Gloucester, President of the African Institution, March 20, 1809.

1811   "On the Right of Great Britain to prevent other Nations from carrying on the Slave-trade".

1811   "A Letter to Henry Brougham, Esq. M.P. on the subject of Reform in the Representation of the People in Parliament", Liverpool.

1811   "On Farm-Leases of the Hundred of West Derby, Liverpool.

1812   "An Answer to a Letter from Mr John Merritt, on the Subject of Parliamentary Reform". Liverpool.

1812   "A Review of the Speeches of the Right Hon. George Canning on the late Election for Liverpool as far as they relate to the Questions of Peace and Reform"

1813   "Lord Nelson's Monument", Liverpool.

1815   "On the Improvement of Chat Moss", Liverpool.

1816   "Catalogue of the Very Select and Valuable Library of William Roscoe", London.

1816   "Catalogue of the Genuine and Entire Collection of Prints, Books of Prints, etc. the Property of William Roscoe.

1817   "On the Origin and Vicissitudes of Literature, Science and Art, and their Influence on the present State of Society"

1818   "A Selection of Psalms and Hymns" edited by Roscoe, Liverpool.

1819   "Observations on Penal Jurisprudence, and the Reformation of Criminals" London.

1819   Catalogue of a Series of Pictures, Illustrating the Rise and Early Progress of   the Art of Painting in Italy, Germany, etc." Liverpool.

1819   Poems by William Roscoe and his Children, Manuscript.

1820   Poems for Youth by a Family Circle, Vol 1. London.

1821   Poems for Youth by a Family Circle, Vol 2. London.

1822   "Illustrations, Historical and Critical of the Life of Lorenzo de Medici called   the Magnificent", with an appendix of original and other documents, London and Edinburgh.

1822   "Memoir of Richard Robert Jones of Aberdaron" London.

1823   "Additional Observations on Penal Jurisprudence, and the Reformation of Criminals", London.

1824 "The Works of Alexander Pope, Esq to which are added a New Life of the Author, an estimate of his poetical character and writings, and occasional remarks" 10 volumes, London

1824 "Fruits of Leisure" Manuscripts.

1824 "Poems Fugitive and Original" Vol 1. manuscripts

1825 "Observations on Penal Jurisprudence and the Reformation of Criminals, Part III in London.

1827 "A Brief Statement of the Causes which have led to the Abandonment of Penitentiary Discipline in the United States. Liverpool.

1828 "Monandrian Plants of the Order Scitamineae, chiefly drawn from living specimens at the Botanic Garden at Liverpool". Atlas folio, issued in parts 1824 to 1828. Liverpool.

Many of Roscoe's publications may be found at the Record Office, Liverpool Central Library. Roscoe was a regular contributor to periodicals including the Gentleman's Magazine, The London Magazine and the Town and Country Magazine.

Books on Roscoe and other Sources of Information

Biographical, Memoirs and Family

Henry Roscoe, The Life of William Roscoe, 1833, 2 volumes, London.

Lucy Aikin,Memoir of John Aikin, 1823 and The Works of A.L. Barbauld, 1825, Liverpool.

George Chandler, William Roscoe of Liverpool, 1953, Bi-centenary volume which includes a selection of Roscoe's poetical works.

Hartley Coleridge, Worthies of Yorkshire and Lancashire, 1836: second edition in 1852, three volumes entitled Biographia Borealis or Lives of Northern Worthies, London.

W.W. Currie, Life Writings and Correspondence of James Currie of Liverpool, London, 1831.

F.W. Dunston, Roscoeana, An Account of the Kinsfolk of William Roscoe and Jane, née Griffies,, his Life, 1905, privately printed.

F. Espinasse, Lancashire Worthies, 1877, London, two volumes.

Washington Irving, The Sketch Book, 1877, 1819-20.

C. Sydney Jones, William Roscoe Centenary Address, Liverpool, 1931.

G.W. Mathews, William Roscoe, A Memoir, London, 1931.

George Murphy, William Roscoe, His Early Ideals and Influence, Liverpool, 1981.

J.D. Passavant, Tour of a German Artist in England (1831) edited by J. Bailey, Wakefield, 1978.

J.A. Picton, Memorials of Liverpool, 1873, Liverpool.

Thomas Traill, Memoir of William Roscoe, Edinburgh New Philosophical Journal, 1832.

James MacKay Wilson, The Border Magazine, Berwick upon Tweed, 1831, Volume 1, Article on Burns and Roscoe.

Manuscript Collections

Roscoe Papers 1 to 5640 covering a period extending from 1771 to his death in 1831, Liverpool City Libraries, Record Office and Local History Department.

A very few Roscoe Papers at the Liverpool Athenaeum.

Historical Works

John Burchard's Diaries, translated by A.H. Matthews, London, 1910.

Edward Gibbon, Miscellaneous Works, 1796, to 1815, Vol.2.

J.E. Graham, The Political Ideas and Activities of William Roscoe, 1787-1801, M.A. Thesis,1970, New Sydney Jones Library, Liverpool University, unpublished.

Francesco Guicciardini, History of Florence, English edition translated by Cecil Grayson, 1964.

J.R. Hale, England and the Italian Renaissance, London, 1954.

Christopher Hibbert, The Rise and Fall of the House of Medici, 1974, London.

Roy Porter, English Society in the Eighteenth Century, London, 1982.

F.E. Sanderson, Liverpool Abolitionists, Liverpool and the Slave Trade and The Structure of Politics in the Eighteenth Century, Liverpool, Transactions of the Historic Society of Lancashire and Cheshire 1972 and 1973.

J.C.L. Sismondi, History of the Italian Republics during the Middle Ages,1809 to 1818.

Nicholas Tenhove, Memoires Genealogiques de la Maison de Medici, translated by Sir Richard Clayton, Bt, London 1797.

G.M. Trevelyan, British History in the Nineteenth Century, London, 1922.

D.G. Weinglass, The Publishing History of Roscoe's Edition of the Works of Alexander Pope, unpublished thesis, Record Office, Liverpool City Libraries, 1969.

The Arts

Michael Compton, William Roscoe and Early Collectors of Italian Primitives, Liverpool Bulletin, Vol.9, 1960-61.

C.P. Darcy, The Encouragement of the Fine Arts in Lancashire, 1760-1860, Manchester, 1976.

Catalogue of Roscoe Collection of Pictures deposited by the Trustees of the Liverpool Institution in the Walker Art Gallery in Liverpool. Preface by M.W. Bracknell.

W. Barnard Faraday, Memoirs and Proceedings of the Manchester Literary and Philosophical Society, 1990, XLIV.

Hugh MacAndrew, Henry Fuseli and William Roscoe, Liverpool Bulletin, Vol.8, 1959-60.
Joseph Mayer, Early Exhibitions of Art in Liverpool, 1876.

Edward Morris, The Formation of the Gallery of Art in the Liverpool Royal Institution, 1816-19. Transactions of the Historic Society of Lancashire and Cheshire, 1992, Vol.142.

Edward Morris, Riches Into Art, Liverpool University Essays.

John Ruskin, Modern Painters, 1843 to 1860, Vol. III.

Giorgio Vasari, The Lives of the Artists, translated by George Bull, Penguin Books, 1965.

Walker Art Gallery, Liverpool, Foreign Catalogue, 1977.

Books, Directories, Articles etc. Relating to Liverpool

James Aspinall, Roscoe's Library, London and Liverpool, 1853.

Peter Aughton, Liverpool, A People's History, Liverpool, 1990.

Margaret Gibson and Susan Wright, Joseph Mayer of Liverpool, London, 1988.

John Hughes, Liverpool Banks and Bankers, Liverpool, 1906.

Leeds Intelligencer, February and March 1824.

Liverpool Directories, 1774, 1777 and 1781.

Gore's Directory of Liverpool.

Liverpool Annals.

Liverpool, Chronicle, January 24, 1829.

Liverpool Daily Post, December 20, 1898.

Miscellaneous

S.A. Allibone, Critical Dictionary of English Literature, 1902, Vol.2.

John James Audubon, Journal, 1826 published 'raw and uncut' by Alice Ford.1967, Norman, Oklahoma.

Robin Boyd, Introduction to Indian Christian Theology, 1969.

Philip Daudy, Les Anglais, London, 1991.

J. Goodier, Chat Moss, Its Reclamation and its Pioneers, a lecture delivered to the Eccles and District History Society, 1970.

Joseph Kastner, A World of Naturalists, London, 1978.

Jeremy Purseglove, The Taming of the Flood, Oxford, 1989.

H. Stansfield, William Roscoe, Botanist, The Liverpool Bulletin, Vol.5, November 1935.

Edward Sackville West, A Flame in Sunlight, London, 1936.

A.R. David and E. Tapp, The Mummy's Tale, Michael O'Mara Books Limited.